THE LITERARY AGENT
AND THE WRITER

THE LITERARY AGENT AND THE WRITER

A Professional Guide

❂❂❂❂

by DIANE CLEAVER

❂❂❂❂❂

Publishers   THE WRITER, INC.   *Boston*

Copyright © 1984
by DIANE CLEAVER

Third printing 1988

Library of Congress Cataloging in Publication Data

Cleaver, Diane.
  The literary agent and the writer.

  Includes index.
  1. Literary agents. 2. Authors and publishers.
I. Title.
PN163.C57 1984   070.5′2   84-5106
ISBN 0-87116-135-4 (pbk.)

Printed in the United States of America

CONTENTS

INTRODUCTION

AN AGENT is a middleman. A man or woman who brings together and stands between an editor and writer. An agent represents writers; he is not a writer or editor, nor can he or she write or publish your manuscript. But an agent will have suggestions and opinions that can make a difference to the writing and publishing of your book. An agent is a negotiator of contracts, responsible for conveying a writer's ideas and representing them fairly and in their best light to publishers. A good agent is a writer's voice in the often conflicting, confusing world of writing and publishing.

Agents place the writers' work with publishers, offer support and advice, and manage the writers' careers and make better business deals for them. But finding one can seem impossible. That doesn't mean you can't find a publisher on your own; it does mean that you must learn to become your own agent.

This book offers information and practical advice about agenting and the business of publishing, what editors look for, and what you can do to give yourself the best chance of finding an editor, having your work read and considered, and being published.

The major problem most new writers have is finding a professional to read their manuscript. Many publishers say they don't read unsolicited manuscripts and that you should have an agent; agents say they are fully committed and can't take on new writers.

The fact is, publishers and agents *are* interested in new writers and new ideas—they're constantly searching for them. There are thousands of people writing and hundreds of manuscripts finding their way to publishers' offices every day. If you don't know what they're interested in, what kinds of manuscripts they want, you are, in effect, sending your manuscript into a vacuum, and the chances are that it will be rejected.

Writers are often unfamiliar with the needs and interests of specific publishers, but as a writer you have to be aware of different publishing companies and what they publish. You should be able to look critically at your own manuscript, just as an editor would, to be aware of the marketplace and the competition. If you can take an objective look at your own manuscript and honestly see a place for it, this book will help you make the right decisions about breaking into the business of publishing.

Publishing and writing are different occupations and while perhaps it shouldn't be so, it is often an adversary relationship. Your book is important to you, but to a publisher your book is one component of a complete list of books composed of dozens of titles he's selling. As an author you have to know something about the marketing of books, how to find the right publisher, how to negotiate, and how to work with an editor. It helps to know how decisions are made, what is actually involved in publishing your book, where it fits in the publisher's scheme of things, what you're up against, and what concerns the publisher.

Because it is difficult to find a publisher or agent, especially with your first manuscript, this book will show you how to be your own agent, or how to find one, how to find the right publisher and editor. It tells you how to write query letters and prepare submissions, and how to present your work in the most professional way. Also, you will find information here about contracts and negotiation, and what happens when your manuscript is bought and published.

THE LITERARY AGENT
AND THE WRITER

I

WHO NEEDS AN AGENT

NOT EVERY writer needs an agent, wants an agent or can find an agent, but as you near completion of your manuscript or proposal, you will begin to think about agents. You will wonder what an agent can do for you, whether you want one or whether you should send your manuscript directly to a publisher and perhaps make your own deal.

Writers often think they should have an agent because they believe publishers will pay more attention to their work if it is submitted by an agent, or because they don't know how to sell it, they don't know publishers or what editors are looking for, they're unfamiliar with contracts and think they'll get a better deal with an agent representing them.

Sometimes, for some writers and some books, these things are true, but as a writer venturing into the marketplace for perhaps the first time, you should know that having an agent does not guarantee publication. It can, and often does, help to be represented, but every agent has stories of books they've believed in and never sold. And, too, there are hundreds of authors

3

who've had bad luck with agents and sold their own work successfully. Many professional writers don't have agents and don't want them. It is possible for new writers with a good idea or a good story to find out about publishing and publishers, to submit their own material, and to sell their work. And, if you're writing poetry or short stories or articles, or if you're a first-time author of a book-length work, it may not be easy to find an agent and you will have to sell your own work directly to the right publishers.

As you begin to think of selling your work, you may decide that you don't need an agent or that you may not be able to find one, and you will plan to sell it yourself. Many writers who do write books and do have agents, submit their shorter pieces—articles and short stories—to magazines on their own. They know their markets, which magazines are interested in what, who will like their ideas.

Most literary agents are set up to sell book-length works, since that's where their major interests lie. Agents do work with magazines, but for the most part, only when they're selling first serial rights—that is, excerpts or chapters of books they represent. Agents tend not to take on writers whose primary interests lie in magazines; they usually don't know the extensive magazine market well enough to be effective, and it takes too much time away from selling books, which are more profitable.

Writers of romances, science fiction, mysteries, and other category fiction for which publishers have special imprints and specific guidelines often don't need agents. Manuscripts in these categories can be submitted directly to publishers by authors; they are read, considered and often bought.

Textbook authors or writers who concentrate in special fields of expertise, such as computers or finance or gardening or crafts, often don't need or want agents, as they are already familiar with the publishers interested in their fields. Most agents are not experts in specific areas, and unless there's a general audience for your book, they will be less enthusiastic about representing it. But a publisher who handles technical books as a matter of course will be eager to hear your ideas and read your manuscript, and will know how to pinpoint your market.

There is also a large number of well-known authors who don't have agents. Judith Guest is one. She completed her first novel and sent it off to the editors at Viking, where it sat with other unsolicited manuscripts waiting to be read. It was eventually plucked out of the "slush" pile by an assistant who liked it and passed it on to a senior editor who bought it. *Ordinary People* was a publishing phenomenon, not only because it was a first novel that sold 102,000 copies in hardcover, was reprinted by Ballantine for a big six-figure advance and made into a movie directed by Robert Redford, but because it was the first time in twenty-eight years that Viking had found a manuscript in its slush pile.

Many authors are interested in the business end of publishing and like the direct contact with their editors through the contract and editorial process. Before launching your manuscript into the world, it will be worth your time and effort to find out something about publishers. Although many large publishers with general trade lists are concentrated in New York, there are major publishers in Boston and on the West Coast, in the South and the Midwest. And there are dozens of medium-sized and small publishers all across the country, some of whom specialize in books of regional interest, or poetry and serious fiction, others in how-to or photography books or technical works. In other words, you don't have to have an agent, or even a New York publisher, to be published happily and successfully.

To sell your own work, you should learn something about the market: Who publishes what kind of book and where your work might be best received. If you've written a romance, you must find romance publishers. If you're a banker and have written a book of financial advice for people with incomes of less than $20,000, don't send a query to a publisher who publishes only popular fiction.

You should also study the competition. What books have you liked in your field, and why? Who published them? Has anyone else written a book on the same subject and if so, what's different about yours? To do this, check the *Subject Guide to Books in Print.* Your local library will have a copy, and you'll see that books are listed by topic rather than title or author. You should also check your local bookstores, see what they have that might be more current, read the book pages of your newspapers and magazines. You want a publisher who is interested in your subject or your kind of novel. You don't want to waste your time going to the wrong publishers, and a little research will help you find the right places to submit your work.

For names and addresses of publishers, consult the *Literary Market Place*. This directory published annually by the R. R. Bowker Company is an essential reference for finding names of publishers, associations, book trade events, conferences, magazine and newspaper publishers and names and addresses of literary agents. It costs $45.00 a year, but you don't have to buy it; your local library will have an up-to-date edition. It might be worth buying every five years or so because it is useful to have the information at your fingertips. You can always bring it up-to-date every year by consulting the copy at your library. The *LMP* also lists the names of editors by publisher. It's important to send a query letter not to "The Editors," but to an individual editor by name. To confirm that an editor's still with a particular company, it's worth a phone call to the publisher; the switchboard will usually give you the information.

If there's a published book you've particularly admired, or if it is in some way related to your own work, it is again worth calling the publisher to find out who the editor of the book was. Then direct your query to that editor. It is not top secret information. It's also a good idea to read acknowledgments in books that you've liked or compare favorably with yours. Authors often thank their editors and agents.

You should definitely subscribe to *Publishers Weekly*, the trade magazine and bible of the publishing industry. It offers book trade news, articles on subjects of interest to publishers and writers, reviews of forthcoming books, information about sales and deals and lots of information about editors and agents, what they've sold or bought. It will give you a good picture and a general knowledge of the publishing industry, what some of its problems are and how it works. It costs $68.00 a year. Your local library will have a recent issue for subscription information. It's a good investment.

So are magazines about writing and publishing, such as *The Writer.* It is specifically directed to writers, has articles about writing and, of great import for writers, precise marketing information about which houses and which editors are looking for what kind of material.

Publishing is a business and as a writer selling your own work you should know something about that business. It can be confusing and overwhelming, but as a writer looking for a publisher you can be successful if you know who the publishers are, what they publish, where they're effective and what their concerns are.

II

HOW TO FIND AN AGENT

IF YOU do decide that you need or want an agent, there are many ways of finding one.

Elizabeth Powers grew up in New Albany, Indiana. Long after she left her hometown she wrote her first mystery novel, *All That Glitters.* She called an old high-school friend living in New York to ask if she knew a literary agent. She was lucky; her friend, who isn't a writer, happened to know one. Elizabeth Powers wrote a query letter outlining her novel and mentioning their mutual friend. The agent asked her to send the manuscript. After some re-working, the manuscript was submitted to publishers and bought by the Doubleday Crime Club.

Gene Bylinsky, author of *Life in Darwin's Universe* and a science writer for *Fortune* Magazine, found his agent on the recommendation of an editor.

Elizabeth Kane Buzzelli, who wrote *Gift of Evil,* heard an agent speak at a writers conference and wrote to her afterwards.

Zoë Kamitses, author of *Moondreamer,* approached her agent on the recommendation of a writer friend.

Jay and Linda Mathews are journalists. I read an article by Jay in the *Washington Post* and wrote to him in Hong Kong where he was stationed. He and his wife, Linda Mathews of the *Los Angeles Times*, transferred to Peking and ultimately wrote *One Billion: A China Chronicle.*

You might not receive a letter from an agent, or know an editor, or have a friend with connections, but you might, as Jessie Ford did *(Love, Remember Me; The Devil's Woman)*, read the name of an agent in a magazine, or go to a conference and find an agent.

There are dozens of writers conferences held at colleges and universities all around the country every year. Some of them are listed in the *Literary Market Place*, many others are advertised locally and in writers' magazines.

Most conferences invite guest writers and editors and agents to speak, and usually time is arranged for personal meetings with students. Sometimes visiting editors and agents will read part of your manuscript, but more important, a conference is a useful place to find out about publishing, what editors are interested in, what is selling well, and who some of the people are in the world of publishing.

If you do attend a conference, the chances are that an editor or agent you meet there will respond to your query requesting him or her to read a proposal or part of your manuscript. I know that I feel an obligation to respond to queries from writers who attended conferences at which I was a guest.

Many colleges and universities have writing programs as part of their curriculum. Find out who heads the program and what the requirements are for taking a course. You may not learn to write in such a course but you will have the opportunity to hear the work and criticism of other writers, as well as your own, and to discuss your ideas with the teachers and others in the class. You will also get information about where to sell, who is looking for what kind of material, and names of specific agents and editors who will read free-lance material. Further, the group offers support and encouragement during the time you are trying to place your work with a publisher or find an agent.

Publishers and agents are open to new writers, but new writers who approach them in a professional manner. If you have some knowledge about what publishers are interested in, who the agents are, and how to present your ideas, it becomes possible to write query letters to publishers and agents (the *Literary Market Place* lists well over 200 literary agents) and to receive a positive response—yes, we will read your manuscript or the beginning chapters; yes, we are interested in knowing more about your work. And what it takes to get that response is not only a good idea or a strong plot, but a well-conceived, professional letter describing your book and asking if the editor or agent to whom you're writing will read it.

III

THE QUERY

When you've completed your book or proposal, you will want a professional to read and consider it. Your first thought will be to pack it up and mail it off to the publisher or agent you've selected to approach, but the way you initially contact these professionals can make the difference between being read or not. Some publishers receive between one and two hundred unsolicited manuscripts a week, and, although it did work for Judith Guest and *Ordinary People,* you don't really want your manuscript to languish in the slush pile. And even then, your manuscript might not be read.

In a survey of twenty publishers—both hardcover and paperback—half of them report that they do not even accept, let alone read, unsolicited manuscripts. They are returned to the sender unopened. All publishers who said that they accepted, and read, unsolicited manuscripts indicated that such manuscripts are handled by assistants who "cut their teeth on the slush pile," and how much attention they paid to these manuscripts depended on their work load. A few pub-

lishers who don't accept unsolicited manuscripts return them with information explaining how to submit
material. And others simply return manuscripts with a
card or note saying thank you but no thank you, and in
that case you don't know whether they've read your
manuscript or not. The following editorial letter ac-
companies the return of unsolicited manuscripts from
Doubleday; most publishers are not so helpful. The
letter explains why your manuscript is being returned
and how to submit and write a query letter:

> Your manuscript was received by Doubleday and is be-
> ing returned unread, for now. Please follow the instruc-
> tions below and we would be happy to review your propo-
> sal.
> The flow of manuscripts into the Doubleday editorial
> offices is so great that our readers are overwhelmed, and
> are therefore unable to give worthy manuscripts the at-
> tention they deserve. We hope that you will understand
> the problem, and that we are still interested in "unsolic-
> ited" manuscripts.
> If you have a manuscript or a partial manuscript you
> wish Doubleday to consider, please follow these important
> steps:
> 1. Write us a letter describing your book. This will be
> read by an editor. If the editor is interested, you will be
> invited to send the manuscript. If not, you will receive a
> rejection letter.
> 2.   Please *do not* send us a manuscript before you have
> had a reply to your letter. Such submissions will be re-
> turned.
> Incidentally, this is a procedure followed by many pro-
> fessional writers. It enables them to get a prompt re-

sponse to their proposal, and saves them the time and expense of sending an entire manuscript to a publisher who might not be interested in it.

HOW TO TELL DOUBLEDAY ABOUT YOUR BOOK

Your letter of inquiry should be addressed to the Editorial Department, Doubleday & Co. Inc., 245 Park Avenue, New York, N.Y. 10017. The letter may be as short as one page, but no longer than six pages (double-spaced). The first sentence should tell us whether your book is a novel, a biography, or whatever. This description should be clear and straightforward. If your book is a novel, please give us an engaging summary of the plot and background, and a quick sketch of the major characters.

If you have already been published, give us details at the end of your letter. You should also tell us of any credentials that particularly qualify you to write your book. For a nonfiction book, it will be helpful to you to consult the *Subject Guide to Books in Print* (available in most libraries) so that you are aware of other books on the same or similar subjects as your own, and can tell us how your book differs from them.

Finally, letters of inquiry should be inviting and typed with good ribbon. If we ask to see your manuscript, it should be submitted double-spaced on white paper. You should retain a carbon copy, since we cannot assume responsibility for loss or damage to manuscripts. Sufficient postage, in the form of loose stamps, should accompany your submission to insure the return of your manuscript in the event it is not accepted for publication.

Editorial Department

The Doubleday information sheet is very clear about submission procedures, and it's an approach that will serve you well with all publishers and agents. Don't send your manuscript; do write a query letter. You will find that people will respond, and often with a request for more information or part of your manuscript.

As you begin to consider your query letter and how you are going to describe your work, you should consider your own proposal or manuscript as a professional might:

What is different about your book?

What is the market?

What is the competition?

Is it a fresh subject, a unique approach?

Are the themes and ideas developed clearly?

Are the motivations and characters developed and integrated effectively within the plot?

Within the framework of your query letter, you will include a description of your book. There is frequently confusion about the difference between a proposal, synopsis, or outline. Often the words are interchangeable and there is no particular form to be followed; the material dictates the form of presentation.

Basically, the proposal is the presentation of the overall idea. If it's nonfiction it might include a chapter-by-chapter outline, a brief description of what each chapter will cover, and a few pages that give an overview of the entire book. The description or overview should explain:

What the book is about.

Facts that support the idea.

What research is completed or planned.

Biographical information which supports the author's authority and reason for writing the book.

If your proposal is for a novel, you will be writing a synopsis of its story line and plot, the series of events that will move the narrative forward. It should introduce the major characters, and describe their relationships and motivations.

An outline is usually more specific about points you plan to cover, whereas a synopsis is usually a general, overall narrative. How proposals are written and prepared is explained in Chapters 4, 5 and 6. First comes the query letter.

A good query letter should be simple and straightforward. It shouldn't be too long. If you've written a novel, your letter should contain a summary of the plot, mention major characters and themes, and background. You should state the length of your manuscript and, if it's relevant, biographical information about yourself. For example, if you've published short stories or articles or published an earlier book, that is of interest to a publisher or agent. If your manuscript is nonfiction, your should establish your credentials, and why you are especially qualified to write it. Include an outline of the contents, your ideas and the points you intend to make, and what will make the book unique.

A query letter, whether it's to an editor or agent, should be:

Authoritative. Whether your proposed book is fiction or nonfiction, show an editor or agent reading your query that you are knowledgeable about the subject and in control of your material.

The synopsis or outline of the book in your letter should reveal the scope of the book. It doesn't have to be written in great detail, but your aim is to convey the essence of the book. An editor or agent wants to be convinced by your letter, to see the marketing potential of your book.

Biographical information should relate only to the specific proposal, your background or writing experience that support the ideas of the book.

Here are three good query letters:

Dear _____

I am a lawyer who specializes in Workmen's Compensation law and Social Security Disability cases. I am in the process of writing a book called *Human Debris: The Injured Worker in America.*

Using case histories and anecdotes about the people involved, my book will expose the fallacies, bureaucracy, and lack of protections for the working men and women of America under the insurance of Workmen's Compensation. The fact is that it is the employer who is protected by Workmen's Compensation and the worker who suffers.

Workmen's Compensation had its first tentative steps in 1907. The Labor Department has recently prepared a comprehensive survey of this employer-financed compensation system. It reveals a program that has strayed from its mandate of paying disabled workers two-thirds of their lost wages.

—Of the estimated 650,000 victims of asbestosis, silicosis and other occupational diseases, only 5% receive workmen's compensation because of Catch-22 provisions of state laws. The few who do get benefits don't get much—an average of one-eighth of their lost income.

—Insurance companies and lawyers are compensated almost as much as the program's intended beneficiaries.

Of the $13 billion paid into the program in 1978, about $5.5 billion—or 42 cents of each dollar—was taken up by administration and legal costs.

—The government now spends billions of dollars a year aiding impoverished workers cast aside by the compensation system—the Social Security's disability insurance program and the welfare system support about five times as many severely disabled workers as does workmen's compensation.

—The number of people crippled by occupational diseases will increase. In the next ten years 500,000 workers are expected to die from asbestos-related diseases. In addition, 85,000 will be disabled by brown lung caused by exposure to cotton dust and 29,000 from silicosis. Very few of these people will get benefits under the present system.

In my book I plan to discuss the bureaucratic problems, the unwillingness of employers to bear responsibility, insurance companies, the doctors and lawyers who work closely with the employers and the workers who are the victims of the system devised to protect them. The victims of the system are not only people suffering from black lung disease and chemical/nuclear-related illnesses: Nurses, clerks, supermarket check-out workers are all vulnerable to certain disabilities because of the work they do.

I have done most of the research for my book, interviewing people in different states—workers, employers, doctors, lawyers, government officials.

If you are interested in my book *Human Debris* I can send you an introductory chapter, proposal and chapter-by-chapter outline. This is a little-explored area which, I believe, would be of interest.

I hope you agree and shall look forward to your response.

Sincerely,

The next query letter is about a novel:

I have just finished writing a novel that I would like you to see with an eye to handling it. It's a big novel. It's big in size—about 175,000 words—and big in scope. It is called *The Big Parade.*

Until now the things I have written haven't been so big but they have been top market. Short stories in *McCall's* and the *Saturday Evening Post,* and a short novel published by Random House.

The novel is complete and ready to send. It's about what has happened in and to America in the last hundred years. It is told in terms of what has happened to the Barondess family, first and foremost its founder Nathaniel Barondess. The family has grown so large, so complex, so multinational, so multifaceted, it is like a projection of the old melting pot in which Nathaniel started as a penniless boy alone. It is like America brought up to date, with all the problems and disillusionments, the ugliness, the over-sophistication and violence that have come with the great rewards.

The wide expanse of time covered in the novel is contained within a contemporary three-day framework, so it has shape as well as grand sprawl.

This framework, this containment, is a current holiday weekend at Seneca Park, Nathaniel Barondess's 1,000-acre Rhode Island estate. As Nathaniel's nine sons and daughters and their spouses and the third and fourth generations, all 96 of them, assemble in his 243-room house, it fills with their loves and hates, their conflicts of financial interest, their prides and jealousies, their acts of violence.

Nathaniel has lived through recent American history, has been part of it all. And in his mind he harbors the haunting ghosts of men and women who created those years and were part of his life. Many of their names are in the history books and in the newspapers, but they are more real in Nathaniel's mind, and he knows what they all must answer for. In the end Nathaniel knows, too, where to turn in placing responsibility.

May I send *The Big Parade* to you?

Sincerely,

The third letter is from a young woman who has been writing short stories and has now begun a novel:

I am writing to inquire about your interest and requirements for representing me.

My writing background is varied in fiction and non-fiction. I won a College Essay Contest for _____ Magazine and wrote a monthly column for one year. My first short story was published in Ishmael Reed's *Yardbird Reader V.*

I am presently a member of the Harlem Writers' Guild and attend the John Oliver Killens Fiction Writing Workshop. Last year I was accepted and attended the Berkeley Writer's Conference. In June of this year, I was a one-month resident at Yaddo Artist Colony in Saratoga Springs.

I am working on a novel. It focuses on a black woman who, after devoting most of her life to raising five children, and having gone through five unsuccessful marriages, is devastated (as many women are) when she finds herself 48 years old and alone without any idea of what she is going to do with the rest of her life. She has a nervous breakdown which she hides from her children, turns to alcohol and valium for companionship and solace, until her children try to help her to accept her new role. She resists these changes because she doesn't feel "necessary" and instead tries to regain her motherly control over each of them by "making trouble." She is frightened and unsure of herself, in much the same way a child entering puberty is, and the story is about her fears and willingness to learn and begin taking her life into her own hands.

Thank you in advance for your time and consideration.

Sincerely,

Most agents and editors will decide when they read your query letter whether they are interested in your idea or story, and in you as a writer. You may not think it's fair, that you may not be able to write a good synopsis or outline and therefore unless an agent or editor reads your complete manuscript, he or she won't be giving you a fair chance, that they can't otherwise tell whether you're good or not. The truth is they can. They can tell whether they like your idea or story, whether it's marketable, if you're competent or an authority, whether your ideas are fresh and whether you're approaching your career as a writer professionally.

Remember, it's easy for an agent or editor to say no, and it's important that your query be positive and direct. Some of the information you consider honest and open or friendly can give negative impressions.

Don't offer the following information:

Your manuscript has been rejected by other agents and editors. Your contact will assume it's a waste of time for him to read it too.

You wrote it several years ago and recently read it again and thought you'd give it another shot. You don't sound like a committed, serious writer.

You have just completed your latest novel but have three more that might be of interest. So, why weren't they published? Past failures are of no interest.

Don't send a handwritten query letter. Type your letter, single-spaced on good paper, use a good ribbon and clean type. Your query letter should be as professional-looking as the manuscript you want to submit.

And never write a letter that reads like this:

> Several years ago I burned out from a positively wild and increasingly hectic career and moved to Arizona at age 60. After a while my ability to bounce back took hold and I began to seriously write. The result is this. I wrote a Novel based on my career. Some of it is so true that I might have to leave the country if it is published. That is in the hands of a Professional Typist, the necessity for which is obvious. (Ha.) My typewriter is ancient and I think we both have arthritis. I have also completed a relatively short story that I'm proud of, since I'd never tried it's type or length before as I tend to write too much. I'm "green" as to the business side of publication, too trusting and got in one mess I'll tell you about when and if necessary. One thing at a time.
>
> I now have some chapters of the Novel. Pure fiction it

THE LITERARY AGENT AND THE WRITER   23

ain't, but you'll never get me to admit that publicly. Which do I send and when? Do I wait for the whole mss. or send what I have?

This letter is badly written, unthinking, unprofessional and asking for rejection. And yet hundreds of query letters in just this vein are written by new writers seeking professional advice. The information it offers is personal and chatty; there is nothing that describes the contents of the manuscript, or even the career on which it is based. It is trying to appeal to the sympathy of the agent or editor on a personal, not professional level, and it's one sure way to be ignored.

An agent or editor wants to know about the book you've written, not how nervous you are, or that you want your book published more than anything in the world. You want to establish a business relationship. You have something to sell and you should present your work without the encumbrance of personal information or gratuitous observations.

Your query shouldn't sound like flap copy: "This is an intensely moving love story." Readers must be free to decide whether it's intensely moving. Some readers will think it is, others won't; personal taste is a real and vital element in the response to your letter. But if it's a clear and straightforward query, it will be taken seriously and considered. *You are not selling yourself; you are selling your manuscript.* If you keep this in mind when you write your query letter you will have taken the first step toward establishing a relationship with an agent or editor.

There is no reason not to submit multiple query

letters. However, they should be addressed and typed individually; they shouldn't be Xeroxed with the salutation written or typed in afterwards. And you should include a stamped, self-addressed return envelope. You might write to ten or fifteen agents and editors and receive perhaps only one request for your proposal or for all or part of your manuscript. Even if you receive two or three positive letters, you should not send your manuscript to more than one editor or agent at a time. It's not fair to the person who asked first and believes that he or she has a clear field. If an editor or agent reads it and then discovers that another editor or agent has it too, he or she might feel, even if he likes it, that he's wasted his time. And, particularly if you're a new writer and actually tell an editor that you're also showing your manuscript to other people, you will evoke negative feelings that will reflect on the manuscript.

If your first query letter brings only negative reactions, re-evaluate your letter. Is it professional? Is it neat? Is your synopsis concise and clear? Are your ideas focused? Is it too long, not complete enough? Did you miss important points? Is it too chatty?

Maybe your query letter reflects some inadequacies in your manuscript; now is the time for you to re-read it. You've been away from it for a while; your eye will be clearer, and you may see some new areas to work on, connections not made, ideas not formed. You may also decide it's still good and still salable, that there's obviously something wrong with your query letter. Perhaps your description of the book isn't clear; or it may be too complicated. You may be trying to explain the whole book rather than concentrating on its essence; or you may have described so many characters that they become confusing.

The point of your query letter is to intrigue an agent or editor. You want someone to say, yes, I'll read fifty pages of your manuscript, or the whole manuscript. Yes, I would like to know more.

Once an editor or agent asks to see your manuscript it is no longer unsolicited and will not become part of the slush pile. When you send either a manuscript, or part of one, in response to a request, there is no need to include a long cover letter with the manuscript. Your initial query letter will be on file, and pulled out when the manuscript arrives. All that is necessary is a brief note reminding the editor or agent that he or she requested the material:

Dear Mr._____,

Thank you for your letter requesting the first fifty or so pages of my novel *At Long Last.* The first three chapters (fifty-three pages) are enclosed. The manuscript is complete. If you would like to see more, I shall be happy to send it. I look forward to your reaction. Thank you.

Sincerely,

Although the editor or agent requested part of your manuscript, he may not get to it right away. If you don't hear within a month remind him with another brief note:

Dear Mr._____,

In response to your request for the first fifty or so pages of my novel *At Long Last* I sent you the first three chapters on _____. I am looking forward to hearing from you.

Sincerely,

You will probably hear from him fairly soon; your note will be enough to jog him along.

IV

PREPARATION

THE WAY YOU present your manuscript or proposal is important. Of course the content is more important, but if your work doesn't look professional, the content may never be considered.

Manuscripts should be typed and double-spaced on good quality paper. Don't use erasable bond for your final copy. The pages stick together, and the type rubs off. Don't use paper so thin that you can see through to the type on the next page. It's distracting to readers. It's quite acceptable to send a Xerox copy, but don't send a carbon.

If you can't type without making lots of mistakes, get a professional to type the final draft. It's worth the financial investment to have your manuscript look professional. Keep good margins. Don't cram the pages with type from side to side or top to bottom. Use a fresh ribbon and change it when it begins to wear, so the type will be clear and readable.

If you use a word processor, it should be printed on a letter-quality printer. Dot matrix is hard on the eyes.

If you're a poor speller, get someone else to check

your copy, or consult a dictionary. Everybody makes spelling mistakes sometimes, but consistently poor spelling can be distracting and annoying, and is the mark of an amateur.

Your manuscript should be clean, professional and easy to read. Agents and editors read hundreds of manuscripts. They don't want it to be a strain to read yours. If it's messy or difficult to read because the type is too light or the page is full of cross-outs or penciled corrections, chances are it won't be read thoroughly. They won't make the effort or take the time; it's not worth it to them. There are too many manuscripts waiting to be read, and it's easier to say no.

Don't put your manuscript in a binder or mail the loose pages in an envelope. If it's a complete, book-length manuscript or a good part of one, send it in a box—the kind that typewriter paper comes in. Binders are cumbersome for a reader to hold and often don't fold back to allow the left-hand side of the typed page to be read. Loose pages not sent in a box can easily be lost. Proposals and sample chapters should be sent in a folder. Your box or folder should always be clearly labeled with your name and the title of your work. Your address should be prominent on both the box and the first page of your manuscript.

When a manuscript arrives in an agent's or an editor's office, it will be logged in, the date of arrival noted, and the title and the name of the author recorded. And then it will sit with other manuscripts waiting to be read. Even with the best precautions, manuscripts may get lost in transit, in the mail room, or even in an agent's or editor's office. Most agents have dozens of manuscripts in their offices at the same time—new ones arriving daily, manuscripts of works in progress, and manuscripts that haven't sold yet—even old manuscripts of books already published. Agents and publishers assume no responsibility for loss of manuscripts, so you should always keep a good, clean copy of your work in a safe place. It is *your* responsibility to do so. Never send out your last copy.

If your manuscript or proposal is well typed and professional looking, an agent or editor can more easily concentrate on the content.

V

NONFICTION SUBMISSIONS

A PROPOSAL IS the overall presentation of your book. Within it, you should include an outline of the proposed book, a description of its contents, your point of view, themes that will be developed, and your conclusions.

Nonfiction is often sold to publishers on the basis of a proposal rather than a complete manuscript. A proposal can take many forms: It can be two pages or one hundred pages; there is no correct length or proper form. If you're a new writer, two pages will probably not be sufficient. Your ideas might be there, but there will be no way for the editor or agent to know that you can actually write the book you propose. Above all, your proposal must be convincing: You must show that you can write, that your ideas and their development are reasonable, and that you have a clear grasp of the material for the book you want to write. In a description or synopsis, you should establish the premise of your book, its focus, who you are and why you are qualified to write it. If you are familiar with the market—with other published books on a similar topic—

point out why yours is different, and suggest the audience potential. Who would buy this book? Who would pay $15 for it? You will also need a chapter-by-chapter outline, and perhaps a brief paragraph explaining what each chapter will cover.

The Path to Pain Control: A Program for Coping by Meg Bogin is a book published by Houghton Mifflin. The proposal for the book was submitted to several publishers, three of whom were interested in making an offer after they'd read it.

Here's the proposal:

THE PATH TO PAIN CONTROL
A Program for Coping

Nobody talks about pain. Like death, it's not what you would call an appealing subject. Unless it hits you, or someone very close to you, chances are you've never given it a moment's thought. Yet at this very moment 40 million Americans are living in the daily hell of chronic pain. And believe me, hell is the right word, though I wouldn't have believed it myself if I hadn't experienced it first-hand. I spent a year and a half waging my own private battle with severe pain as the result of an incapacitating muscle disease, doing my best to tough it out alone and keep my suffering to myself. There wasn't a decent book in sight I could turn to for advice or solace. Of course I knew I wasn't the only person in pain; I knew that there were people much worse off than I. But not until I started work on *The Path to Pain Control* did I become aware of the staggering dimensions of the problem.

With more than twenty million Americans suffering from arthritis, ten million from migraines, seven million from serious back pain and millions from injuries sustained in accidents and wars, not to mention those afflicted with other painful conditions (ulcers, kidney stones, colitis, ileitis, neuro-muscular disorders, sickle cell anemia, hemophilia, etc.), chronic pain plagues 1 in 6 Americans—more than the number of insomniacs. I'm talking about 40 million people, *a population of chronic sufferers the size of the combined populations of the nation's seven largest cities—New York, Los Angeles, Chicago, Philadelphia, Detroit, San Francisco and Washington, D.C.*

Learning to live with pain is the most challenging life experience I have ever had to face. It is a process that demands the utmost in imagination and flexibility, qualities we all possess to a greater or lesser degree but which few situations test so dramatically. As a writer used to the insecurities of a free-lance life I thought of myself as a person who knew how to live from day to day; who knew how to roll with the punches, how to improvise and invent. I thought imagination and flexibility were my specialty. It turns out I couldn't have been more wrong. After a year and a half of trying to free myself from pain I was in more pain than ever. Instead of outwitting pain, it had outwitted me. I had run through all the non-addictive painkillers and was ready for morphine. I was in checkmate. On the brink of addiction, I realized it was time for me to take a closer look at my relationship to pain.

This book grew out of that realization. By making pain my project—by reading, researching, interviewing and keeping a daily record of my observations and reactions—I developed a coherent plan that enabled me to dramatically reduce my pain and cope successfully with the new lowered level I had reached. Finally I can breathe a sigh of relief. I am no longer a pain "victim." I've turned the tide, and I'm convinced that if I could do it any man or woman can.

The Path to Pain Control is a self-help book that gives people in pain a comprehensive, practical plan for dealing with the day-to-day and long-term management of chronic pain. Geared for mass-market sales, it is the first down-to-earth, realistic, step-by-step approach to living with pain. As one of the millions who have suffered chronic pain, I know from personal experience the physical and mental anguish of unabating pain and the difficulty of learning to cope with it. I also know how eagerly people in pain snap up any book that promises help—and how time after time they are let down by the shallowness, if not downright dishonesty, of authors who promise help but fail to deliver.

I learned the hard way that pain cannot be "killed." What I *have* found is that severe pain can be dramatically reduced by eliminating the compounding factors each of us brings to the experience of pain. *The Path to Pain Control* systematically explores all these "extras"—fear, anxiety, uncertainty, medical ignorance, dependency, familial and cultural attitudes toward pain—so that the reader will be able, as I was, to get down to the barest minimum of pain caused by his/her actual medical condition. Once that minimum has been reached, coping becomes the key word. The book presents a whole range of options for coping, using self-help exercises to show readers how to find the orientation and techniques best suited to individual personalities and medical conditions. Thus, essentially the book can be divided into two stages. First, learning to reduce pain to the lowest possible level for each person—*pain control*. Second, once this new lower level has been reached—*coping*.

Most published books on pain are written by "experts" (doctors, psychiatrists, even stuntmen). *The Path to Pain Control* shows that the only experts on pain are people in pain themselves. Because each of us perceives pain differently, learning to cope with it depends on knowing exactly what makes our own pain "tick"—how to *read* our pain. By taking your pain apart, the book explains, you can—as I have—put yourself back together again.

The Path to Pain Control guides the reader through a logical series of self-assessment techniques that shows each individual how to develop his/her own pain plan. Beginning with a chapter called "Taking Your Pain Apart . . . So You Can Put Yourself Back Together," the book moves from the general to the particular, interweaving medical data, case histories (including my own), attitudes toward pain in other cultures, the wisdom of various religious practices and forms of meditation, the journals and writings of famous people who have lived with pain, as well as interviews with average people in pain and those who treat them. Dozens of practical exercises and techniques are built into this rich context of ideas to sharpen the reader's awareness of how pain functions in his/her life. This self-knowledge is the ultimate goal of *The Path to Pain Control.* By following the book's progression, the reader becomes his/her own expert on pain. This is a self-help book in the truest sense of the word. Readers will not only find ideas that are useful to them but will learn how to invent their own techniques and find their own paths to pain control.

Major topics covered include: personal determinants of pain (family history, age, sex, ethnic background, religious beliefs, economic status, etc.); relationships with family and friends; the pros and cons of pain-killers; alternate modes of analgesia (acupuncture, massage, hypnosis, biofeedback); new forms of group support (group therapy, healing services, co-counseling, pain clinics);

techniques for coping—a whole chapter of suggestions with step-by-step guidelines for how to invent your own. The emphasis of the book is on how to convert pain "energy" into life "energy."

The past five years have witnessed a groundswell of new interest in pain as a major health issue, beginning with the founding of the International Association for the Study of Pain in 1975 and followed by the creation of the American Pain Society in October 1977 and the Interagency Committee on New Therapies for Pain and Discomfort (under the aegis of the National Institutes of Health) in December of the same year. This same period has seen a parallel media boom. Between March 1959 and March 1976 *Readers' Guide to Periodical Literature* showed an average of five articles a year on pain, all of them in the popular science magazines. In 1976–77 there were nine, with *Vogue* represented three times. In 1977–78 there were eight, with *Mademoiselle, McCall's, Newsweek* and the *New York Times Magazine* joining the ranks of the science publications. But it is over the past 14 months from March 1978 to the present that a phenomenal jump has taken place: as of May 1979 there have been 21 articles on pain, with *Good Housekeeping, Saturday Review, Better Homes and Gardens, McCall's, Vogue, Harper's Bazaar, Christianity Today, Business Week, New York Magazine,* the *New York Times Magazine* and *America* outstripping the science media. Obviously, magazine editors are "onto" the fact that millions of their readers are in pain. Yet the gist of almost every one of these articles is that the problem of pain is still just that—a problem.

A handful of books on pain has appeared in recent years, all of them wide of the mark. Either they are written by doctors, who unfailingly "push" their own special clinics or therapies and talk down to the reader from the heights of their technical "expertise"*—how many of them have been in the pain person's skin?—or else they are personal accounts (How I Conquered Pain, Victory Over Pain, etc.) that generally turn out to be vague testimonies of religious revelation that may have helped one particular author but offer little concrete help to anyone else.

The best of the recent books is *The Politics of Pain,* by Washington-based health writer Helen Neal (McGraw-Hill, 1978), a fact-packed, well-argued plea for a federally backed nationwide research program on pain. *Publishers Weekly,* going on to cite the figure of 40 million in chronic pain, opens its favorable review with, "There's a ready-made market for this excellent book about pain." But *The Politics of Pain* is *about* pain, not *for* people in pain—as *Library Journal* states, it is "not a manual for sufferers." Obviously written with health planners and politicians in mind, only 7500 hardcover copies were printed—hardly a book for mass consumption. The book has its place, but until the nation's policy-makers produce a coordinated policy on pain, where does it leave people in pain? Nowhere. *There simply does not exist a single book they can turn to for help in the day-to-day struggle with pain. The Path to Pain Control* was conceived to meet this critical need.

The Path to Pain Control uses no gimmicks; it pushes no special clinics, drugs, "latest techniques" or religious awakenings. It is a no-nonsense book for the millions of pain victims who have had it with being preyed on by self-righteous doctors or the quack purveyors of empty promises (see *Life Without Pain* by Komar, self-styled Houdini,

---

*see *Pain: A Personal Experience,* by J. Blair Pace, M.D. (Nelson-Hall, Chicago, 1976) and *Coping With Chronic Pain,* by Nelson Hendler, M.D. and Judith Alsofrom Fenton (Clarkson N. Potter, New York, 1979).

Berkley Books, 1979). Because of their desperation, people in pain are a virtually guaranteed market. (Sad testimony to this are the almost weekly headlines on pain "miracles" in the *National Enquirer,* the country's number one weekly paper with a circulation of 5,200,000.) It is time they had easy, economical access to a book of real quality—a clear, readable, practical book that treats the reader with respect from the very first page. *The Path to Pain Control* can be that book.

While written primarily for people in pain themselves, the book will also be of interest and use to their families, friends and co-workers. There is a special chapter ("Pain-free Relating") for those closest to people in pain—the loved ones who suffer their own, often unrecognized kind of pain: the helplessness of onlookers, the anguish of dramatic and unexpected life changes (such as economic hardship), even anger and resentment when pain creates a barrier between them and someone they love.

In addition, *The Path to Pain Control* could be an indispensable tool for the millions of professionals involved in the health services—doctors, nurses, social workers, psychologists, psychiatrists, physical therapists and those engaged in alternate forms of healing. With courses in pain beginning to make their way into the catalogs of nursing and medical schools across the country, the book could become required reading for those now preparing to enter the health professions.

The nation's half-million doctors annually write more than 100 million prescriptions for pain-killing drugs, at a cost to consumers of some $800 million dollars. And Americans spend an additional $2 billion a year on non-prescription analgesics. Yet chronic pain, as both patients and doctors know all too well, eludes even the strongest pain-killers. Despite new research, despite pain clinics,

chronic pain is still one of this country's most distressing
medical problems (some say #3, after heart disease and
cancer). What's more, with longer life expectancies and a
growing senior citizen population, the number of people
exposed to pain-producing conditions and diseases is continuing to grow. All the more reason for a book like *The
Path to Pain Control,* which can help where even doctors
have no answers.

There is every reason to assume that with minor up-
dates *The Path to Pain Control* could be kept in print
through numerous editions. Reader response is likely to
be of considerable volume and could greatly enrich suc-
cessive printings. Now that media interest has reached
unprecedented levels, serial rights are a strong possibility.
So are foreign sales; the book's level-headed, inter-
disciplinary approach should have wide appeal throughout Europe and Latin America.

Not all nonfiction proposals have to take exactly this
form, but this proposal contains, as every proposal
should, the premise and focus of the book; it tells you
what the book will cover, how the ideas will be developed and what they're based on. It conveys who the
author is, why she wants to write this book and her
qualifications for doing so. It is well-written, intelligent, well-conceived and, as she points out, the only
book about pain that she knows of written not by a
doctor or therapist but by someone experiencing
chronic pain.

It is an entirely convincing proposal. Meg Bogin obviously knows her subject thoroughly and intimately.
Editors reading it could clearly see that she did not
intend to write her *personal* story, which would be less

interesting, but that she intended to write about pain and coping with it. She would be writing *out* of her experience but not *of* her experience.

A table of contents followed these first eight introductory pages.

THE PATH TO PAIN CONTROL:
A Program for Coping

Author's Preface
Preface by Herbert A. Schreier, M.D.
Acknowledgments
Introduction

PART I
1. TAKING YOUR PAIN APART . . . SO YOU CAN PUT YOURSELF BACK TOGETHER
2. LEARNING TO LISTEN: YOUR PAIN MAY BE TRYING TO TELL YOU SOMETHING
3. TURNING PAIN ENERGY INTO LIFE ENERGY
4. SETTING NEW GOALS

PART II
5. COPING: A WAY OF LIFE
6. TO TAKE OR NOT TO TAKE: THE PROS AND CONS OF PAIN-KILLERS
7. PAIN-FREE RELATING: HOW TO KEEP CLEAR IN PAIN AND LOVE
8. PAIN SURVIVAL KIT: SPECIAL TECHNIQUES FOR DEALING WITH SEVERE PAIN

Suggested Reading
Index

Chapter descriptions, a paragraph for each chapter (six more pages), followed the table of contents:

Chapter 1: *Taking Your Pain Apart . . . So You Can Put Yourself Back Together*

> This chapter presents one of the central ideas of the book—that pain control is not a magical process but a rational one. Taking responsibility for your own pain is the main theme. The latest medical and psychological research on pain, along with ethnologic studies on pain tolerance in different cultures, will be presented to give the reader a sense of pain as a controllable phenomenon. Because pain is perceived both in the body and the mind, the chapter stresses the importance of separating the objective (physical) and subjective (psycho-social) determinants of pain. Goal: reducing both to lowest possible levels.

This package, containing fifteen pages, was the initial proposal that I received from Meg Bogin.

She had written an earlier book *(Women Troubadors)* but *The Path to Pain Control* was her first book aimed at a specific but general audience. Editors did not know Meg Bogin's work or her writing, and I felt it was important to give a sense of her style and the tone of the book. Rather than beginning with chapter one, I suggested that she write an introductory chapter, which could later be used as the basis for the introduction to her book. This would tell editors, and eventually readers, more about her own experience with pain: When it began, how it evolved, treatments she'd undertaken and her evolution to the point at which she could stand outside her own chronic pain to write this book, one which offered a clear-cut program that anyone who suffered chronic pain could use.

The sample introductory chapter she wrote was nineteen pages long and confirmed the initial proposal: that she had something valuable to say about pain, that she had practical advice and well-researched information, that she could write it objectively, and that she would write it well.

The "package" for *The Path to Pain Control* was submitted to publishers in the form presented here. Although in a book the table of contents would be placed at the beginning, in the proposal—which in effect all of this material is—the initial description of the book comes first, then the table of contents, and then the introductory chapter. The description is important because it should draw an editor's interest right away. If that works, the table of contents becomes interesting. If you begin with the table of contents, it will usually be passed over anyway until the editor has read the description of what this book is about.

A proposal, as an indicator of a book, has to have its own personality. Behind the writing, whatever the subject, the reader needs to sense the writer, his point of view, his expertise, his experience. You might be writing a book about the stock market, a political analysis of South American politics, a how-to book, a true story about something you've experienced; whatever, it has to assume its own identity, has to be larger in scope than your own experience.

And finally, you'll have to consider if your book is good enough—good enough to compete in the marketplace, good enough to get some attention, good enough in style and content. As a writer it's a question you'll have difficulty answering about your own work, but it's the first to be considered by agents and editors. "Good enough" involves a lot of elements: style, your ability to present ideas, the point of view, conclusion— all these things add up to good enough or not. There are many different opinions, even among professionals, about what is "good enough." An agent can send a manuscript to ten publishers and get ten reactions that range from rejection to an offer. Everyone's opinion is valid, and if you can stand back from your work a bit, yours is too.

A good proposal, like Meg Bogin's, conveys a great deal of information beyond the obvious facts. It's why three publishers wanted to buy her book, and it's why it was published.

VI

SUBMITTING FICTION

UNLESS YOU'RE an established fiction writer, selling a novel on a proposal and a chapter or two is difficult, if not almost impossible, in today's marketplace. It's often easy to write a good beginning to a novel; the difficulty is completing it. Editors know this and are cautious about committing themselves at this stage. And frankly, they don't have to. There are enough complete manuscripts and proposals being submitted by agents and established novelists so that there is little reason for them to take chances on sample chapters and a synopsis by an unknown writer. If you're a first-time novelist, I strongly urge you to be well into your novel before querying either agents or publishers. *Publishers are buying books, not ideas.*

Although publishers rarely make commitments on the basis of sample chapters and a synopsis from a new writer, that is often what they'll ask to see first if they are intrigued by your query letter. If these sample chapters live up to the quality of your query, they will then ask for the rest of the manuscript.

Whether it's your first novel or your fifth, you do

need support and encouragement as you write your novel. You want a professional to have faith in you. But the first leap of faith has to be made by you. You have to believe that you have a good story to tell, that you will complete it, and that it will be good. If you don't have this conviction, if you aren't well launched into the book before you query publishers, the chances are that no one else will have faith in your story either.

A classic approach in writing a popular novel is for the author to write the first two chapters and back them up with a plot synopsis and sketches of the major characters. A synopsis is like an outline; it gives the general form of the book. It should be written in a straightforward narrative to highlight the major plot points and major characters. Don't write a chapter-by-chapter outline for a novel. This tends to get flat and boring and have a "and then this happens, and then that happens" tone. The straight narrative overview of your novel should be enticing enough to encourage a reading of the manuscript.

Your synopsis can be strengthened with character sketches of major characters. They can give further background on characters mentioned in the synopsis, may reinforce plot points, and introduce new elements that weren't mentioned in the synopsis of your novel. John Foreman's proposal for S, which sold to Fawcett and was published under the Ballantine/Fawcett imprint, included the first two chapters of his book—about thirty pages—a twenty-one page synopsis of the entire novel, and character sketches. Here is a sketch of one of the leading characters, Kay Bright:

Publisher, editor-in-chief, and presiding genius of *S* Magazine, Chairman of the Board and principal stockholder of Brighten (a.k.a. Bright Enterprises, Inc.), Kay Bright is gorgeous, talented, innovative, ambitious and witty. She is a major force in international fashion because of the pervasive influence of her magazine.

S is Kay's personal creation, a magazine she virtually single-handedly brought from obscurity (as a wholesale manufacturers' catalogue) into international prominence as the premier fashion forum.

Kay Bright has an uncanny eye for taste trends. She also has the sort of striking appearance that makes people stop and look. Her magazine grosses higher advertising revenues and has a wider circulation than any other fashion periodical in the country—or the world. *S* publishes French and Italian editions already and talks are under way for a possible German edition. The gossip in its columns is the juiciest; the photo spreads are works of art; the editorial content, especially the interviews of world personalities, is widely acknowledged to be brilliantly written and perceptive. Kay socializes with a jet set and is the subject of a good deal of gossip herself. Particularly her spectacular romances, the most recent of which is with America's number one male box office attraction, Robert Bradshaw.

Kay comes from a big family firmly rooted in the suburban lower middle class. Her parents love all their children, but they do not really approve of successful women. Her mother, acknowledged as a "saint" by everyone who knows her, is convinced that Kay is headed for loneliness and old age as a spinster. Her father believes that no respectable man would ever marry a business tycoon. Although he is not a mean man, Kay's father has the ability to hurt her deeply with his comments on her life and where it's going. He also might be just a little jealous, although his jealousy is on a level he'd never consciously admit.

Kay is brilliant and charming, but selfish and head-strong too. Indeed, she's had to be that way in order to get where she is. She's had a mentor, an older man who perceived her talents and was in the position to help her career at a critical point. He was the real impetus behind her entry into publishing. But it was her own talent that carried Kay through a difficult childhood, through a miserable and stormy adolescence, through multiple destructive love affairs, to the pinnacle of success she occupies today.

Kay is strong. She's a general, and S is her fortress. In the late 1960s, she goes public with her magazine, and in the process creates a corporation that now controls various lucrative publishing interests, in addition to the magazine, and a rapidly growing designer licensing division. But Kay is crucially dependent on tangible evidence of her own success. She's one of those outwardly impervious characters who deep down is really terribly insecure, both as a woman and as a person of substance and worth. She constantly strives to produce hard irrefutable evidence of her solidarity, talent and formidability.

Kay leads a flashy media-oriented New York City existence. Her brownstone duplex apartment has been photographed for *Architectural Digest.* She lives alone, except for her Jamaican maid. There is a voluble Puerto Rican super and a cat named Rudy Vallee also consistently on the domestic scene.

John Foreman's novel S is about a corporate take-over. The plot synopsis outlines the story, introduces the major characters, their conflicts and resolutions. The character sketches give background which, as the novel is written, is woven into the nature and structure of each character. If you try to do this in the plot synopsis, it can become cumbersome and too long. By separating the two major elements—plot and character—a proposal for a popular novel can be simpler and more straightforward.

Another example is found in Andrew Coburn's novel, *The Babysitter*. When he planned *The Babysitter*, Andrew Coburn already had several published novels to his credit. Because of his track record, he was able to submit only a five-page synopsis of his book to his publisher, W.W. Norton. It does give the basic situation—a very simple idea, but a very real and frightening one—and introduces, very briefly, the major characters:

Synopsis of *The Babysitter*

After a movie and a bite at Brigham's, John and Hannah Wright drove through dark, tepid heat to their suburban home, where they expected at least one light burning—if not in their daughter's room then certainly in the den, where the babysitter, a college student, spread her books.

The house was black.

John Wright pawed a switch, lit the front hall, and saw blood on his fingers, some on the wall, and more on the floor. He tried to block his wife, force her back, but she was bolted in place and screaming in his ear.

The sitter lay in the light.

Her head was no longer whole. It had been beaten,

battered, front and center. Her hair was gore. Her eyes were open, popped, stained. Her mouth was twisted, as if her teeth wanted to come out. Her shirt was ripped open, and her breasts were bare but unmarked, as though the killer had simply been curious and probably tender with them. Her jeans were secure.

Hannah Wright was tottering now. She was still screaming but without sound, for she had stuffed a fist in her mouth. She was choking on it. John Wright had to wrench it out, and he had to slap her to stop her from doing it again. She did not seem to feel the blow.

"The baby," she said in a voice so hoarse it sounded like somebody else's. Tearing her eyes from the body, she started for the stairs. He grabbed her.

"Let me."

They both went. Toward a room they did not want to enter. He, tilted backwards, illuminated it. She gasped. No child in the crib, no blood on the blanket, no signs of slaughter, nothing except a deathly quiet, as if their daughter had never existed.

So begins their horror: the seemingly senseless murder of their sitter and the abduction of their fourteen-month-old daughter—but for what purpose? They are not wealthy, powerful or famous. They have friends and acquaintances, no enemies, no association with criminals, no contact with crazies. He sells ad space for a struggling weekly, and she teaches, eighth-grade, public school. She goes to pieces, and he would have if she had not done so first.

No clues, no ransom demand, no communication at all from the kidnapper. Only flurries of policemen, state, federal and local. Uncontrollable droves of people from the media, and phony phone calls of the cruelest kind. Endless questions, most of them revolving around the dead sitter, who becomes the biggest mystery of all, for nothing about her checks out, as if she had been her own fantasy, her own creation. A very young woman, quietly efficient, vaguely sad, noticeably introverted, who told lies within lies, fabricated her family and friends and so becomes a phantom in death, buried under a name that could not have been hers: Paula Aherne.

The frustration of the investigators is summed up when a burly state detective, who has no respect for the locals and less for the Feds, pounds his fist on John Wright's kitchen table and shouts, "Who the fuck was she?"

The core of the novel is John Wright's solitary search for the identity of Paula Aherne, which instinct tells him is the only hope he has of finding his daughter, who he is certain still breathes, still laughs, still clutches to life. He cannot believe otherwise and stay sane.

He talks to people who have already been questioned and requestioned, haunts places she had been to, interrogates everybody, makes a nuisance of himself. The search takes him to a professor who did not even know she had been in his class. To a rest room in a singles' bar, where her name is gouged into a wall. To a telephone booth where his unlisted number is scratched on the metal shelf. To men who may have known her and abused her physically. To an Italian coffee shop with a large espresso machine, whose silver surface is brilliantly reflective. She used to gaze at herself in it, he is told, and he too stares into it, as if expecting to see her.

The heat of the hunt. He's sweating now as he searches because he feels that he's getting closer, that he is hearing echoes of her, as if she were hollering to him, trying to help him. He is picking up things on her the police have not, and he is receiving a picture of her, maybe a true one, of a girl who was born fragile, vulnerable, who had a horrible childhood and was on her own before she was of age, who protected herself by staying secretive—stepping sideways instead of forward, sticking to the shadows, covering her tracks. Who all her life feared something or someone.

And as he gradually unravels the mystery of who she was, nearly losing his life in the process, he draws nearer and nearer to his daughter.

The novel concludes with John Wright tracking his daughter to a tenement and finding her alive and well, in the overly tender care of a middle-aged woman who claims the child is hers and honestly believes it. A woman who has spent time in institutions and has scarred wrists and a nose dented by a long-ago blow. Paula Aherne's mother. Also her murderer.

Being able to write a synopsis, in whatever form is appropriate for your work, is important. It should give the sense and style and story, but you should also think of it as a selling device. You want whoever reads it to be intrigued, to want more. Writing a synopsis is not writing the novel; you have to take the high points and weave them into a short, coherent piece that stands alone. Even if you have a complete novel ready to show, it is in your best interest to have a synopsis to submit to an agent or an editor.

Other than "big" books and literary novels, one area of fiction that remains quite steady is the category novel—romances, westerns, male adventure, and mysteries that for the most part follow fairly strict formulas. They usually run from 55,000 to 65,000 words in length, following pretty closely "rules" or "guidelines" set by the publishers. The romance novel publishers—Harlequin, Silhouette, Candlelight Ecstasy, Berkley/Jove, for example—offer guidelines to authors interested in submitting their manuscripts to them. Here's the beginning of a sample guideline for Berkley/Jove's Second Chance at Love series:

> *PLOT:* The plot is the love story of the heroine and the man who is her "second chance at love." Her first relationship must have been serious enough for her to have felt she was in love and committed, and it must have ended before the start of the novel. The heroine can be a divorcee, a widow, or perhaps jilted for a reason that does not reflect badly on her. Or she may have become disillusioned about men and be devoted to her career, or have had family responsibilities. These are, of course, only some of the possibilities—creative twists are welcome.
>
> The hero "Mr. Right" (the second love) is introduced in the first chapter—in fact, the closer to page one, the better! *The new romance* is the subject of the book, but the heroine's background has to be included in the story. Despite the conflicts and complications between the heroine and hero, the story is upbeat in tone. A light touch is all-important in the treatment, since these novels provide readers with an escape from their real-life dilemmas. Therefore, controversial social issues (nuclear power, right to life, etc.) and serious personal problems (alcoholism, mental illness) are to be avoided. Elements of suspense/intrigue and gothic touches are not permitted—for example there are no kidnapping, blackmail, or murder schemes in *Second Chance at Love* novels. We're always looking for work that is witty, as well as very sensual and

romantic. Humorous situations and clever dialogue require skillful handling, but can help maintain a light tone and make the story very entertaining.

In brief, then, a *Second Chance at Love* author must create a heartwarming and exciting love story. The writer's job is to get the heroine and hero together, keep them together, make sparks fly, put obstacles in the path of true love, and finally resolve the complications and the story on a high note with a satisfying ending.

The "tip" sheet goes on to explain in great detail what the heroine and hero should be like, situations that are of interest to them. All romance lines have somewhat different requirements. There are many variations, and if you want to write romances, you should write to publishers for their guidelines. Romance lines are open to new writers, and you don't need an agent to have your manuscript considered. If you're a first-time novelist, the editors like to see your complete manuscript, but even if you submit only the first two chapters and a synopsis of the rest of your novel, it will be considered. If they like your material, the editors may not offer you a contract right away, but they will encourage you and work with you toward completion of your novel.

The publishing market has changed. There's not as much money to spend, and fiction—always a difficult marketplace—is harder to break into than ever; publishers are looking for "big" books or literary books, or strict category books.

"Big" books are basically books that have a shot at the bestseller lists. If you look at the bestseller lists, you'll see that most of the authors on it are not first-time writers. They're brand-name writers like Sidney Sheldon, Judith Krantz, Stephen King, Anne Tyler, John Updike, or Danielle Steel. The books are large in scope, large in ideas and character, or are books by established literary authors whose readership has grown through several books and increasing critical attention.

The bestseller lists in *The New York Times Book Review* are the national indicator of how well books in both hardcover and softcover are selling. It isn't a scientific method of establishing sales, but each week *The New York Times* calls key stores across the country to ask what's selling that week. If a bookstore has a pile of Judith Krantz novels in stock, that's what they're selling or want to sell, and that's what they report.

Getting books into the bookstores is a problem. The publishers' sales representatives visit bookstores months before books are published. If you're an established author, a store will buy more copies based on past experience. If you're an unknown writer, it's more of a gamble. The publishers' sales representatives won't force stores to take more books than they think they can sell.

Unlike the situation in other businesses and products, there's a refund policy on books, and depending on the discounts offered by publishers to bookstores, a publisher might have to give a full refund on returned books. If a book doesn't sell, the bookstore returns it to the publisher for a full or partial refund. Although the publisher's aim is to keep returns at a minimum, the reality is that on the average, approximately 50% of the books ordered by and shipped to the bookstores are returned because they are not selling. This means that the returned copies go back to the warehouse for a while. But warehouse space is expensive, so if the books don't move out to fill new orders, they are remaindered, or sometimes destroyed, if there's not enough profit in the remainder price offered. Remaindered books are sold in bulk to companies specializing in buying and selling remainders. They are bought from the publishers at a minimum price and sold well below cost to bookstores and other outlets that in turn sell them at a deep discount. There's little money and no royalties for authors in remainder sales. It's a costly procedure for both the publisher and the writer, and, therefore, publishers want to be confident that the books they publish have a reasonable sales expectancy, whether that is 10,000 or 100,000 copies for individual titles. The aim is to sell books, not to have them returned, and certainly not to have to remainder them.

The novels that are much harder to sell are the good, middle-range novels that are serious in intent but have no outstanding literary merit—especially if they are by unknown or little known writers. And that, sadly for most writers, is where so many novels fall. To a publisher such a novel offers no compelling reason for publication. It will probably sell fewer than 7,000 copies, often a lot fewer, and there won't be any major reviews on which to build the author's future reputation. There's no profit or glory in publishing novels that won't sell well enough to break even.

Publishing a book is expensive. The author's advance is the least of it and the costs are basically the same on every book. Whether you receive an advance of $75,000 or $7,500 (or less), the overhead on producing your book is the same. Whether the publisher plans to print 10,000 or 100,000 copies (where the cost of paper makes a difference), there are fixed overhead costs in producing your book—the editor's time, production, manufacturing, jacket design, promotion and sales, office overhead all adding up to about $40,000 or $50,000 before even one copy of a book is in the stores.

These figures can be discouraging, but as a writer, you should be aware of what you're up against and how best to present your work so that, in turn, an agent and publisher can see its value and possibilities.

VII

WHEN YOU HAVE AN AGENT

IF YOUR QUERY letter works—that is, if you've presented your book in an intriguing, informative manner—the day will come when your stamped, self-addressed envelope is returned with a letter from an agent that says, "If you'll send me your manuscript, I'll be happy to read it."

Agents are like editors; they want only what they ask to read. If fifty pages are requested, send fifty pages or so. Don't send fifty pages that end in the middle of a chapter or a sentence or an incomplete idea. Send forty-five or sixty pages, wherever there's a natural break. If an agent requests a table of contents and a sample chapter, that's what you should send.

Even though an agent has expressed interest in your book, don't send the complete manuscript if it's not requested; doing so will only evoke a negative response. As a new writer, you may think that by sending an agent a complete manuscript he or she will simply read as much or as little as he wants. But it doesn't work that way: It gets put aside. Agents' priorities are with the clients they already have, with the problems that come up each day, with new deals and contract negotiation. Reading has priorities, too; first an agent will read the manuscripts of authors he or she already represents, then those by authors who've been recommended by other writers or editors, and, finally, manuscripts from unknown writers.

I nearly always ask for a chapter or some pages when I read a query letter that interests me. I don't want to commit myself to the time it will take to read a complete manuscript until I know more about it. If I've received the number of pages or chapters I've requested, I can usually respond within a week or two. A complete manuscript will be put aside until there's time.

The first fifty pages—or a couple of chapters and an outline—that I ask for following a query are enough to indicate to me whether you can write the book or whether it's an idea that's just not going anywhere. If it doesn't work for me, I'll send it back; if it does, I'll ask for the complete manuscript. If I find the manuscript well-conceived, well-written, and intriguing, if I think it's salable, the chances are that I will want to represent it. And then you'll receive a letter from me, saying why I like your manuscript, where I think it could use a little work, and telling you something about me and our agency and that I would like to represent your book.

When an agent writes or phones and offers to represent you, your impulse will be to cheer and say yes. But remember, while the agent knows quite a lot about *you* through your manuscript, you probably know nothing about him or her. Although you may be prepared to take this agent on faith, you don't have to say yes right away.

If you live in the same city as the agent, it will be easy to set up a meeting and talk. If you are separated by hundreds of miles, your business will be conducted by letter and over the phone. If you live at a distance, you might do well in the initial stages of your relationship to communicate with your prospective agent by letter. It's too easy to say yes to a persuasive, enthusiastic, eager voice telling you how terrific your manuscript is, and what plans he or she has for selling your book. This is a business, a fiduciary relationship; no one is doing you any favors, and you should have questions. Don't be too beguiled by a lovely phone conversation, only to think of a dozen questions once you've hung up.

1. *Listen to what the agent says about your work.* Do you like what he's saying? Does his vision of your book jibe with yours? Does he have too many reservations, too many suggestions for major changes? Do you believe those changes will make your book clearer or stronger? Would those changes strengthen or weaken the intent of your book? Do you and the agent see eye to eye on your work?

Agents often do make editorial suggestions for changes that they want you to make before they approach publishers. When I read a manuscript, I can see where it can be strengthened and improved, where an idea is not clear, areas that raise questions rather than give answers. I discuss these points with authors and, if we agree, the author will do additional work. I am not always right. If an author can point out something I've missed, the reason for his points, I am willing to change my mind. And authors, too, are usually prepared to do more work if I make a good case for my suggestions.

Occasionally, an author will not want to do more work before the book is sent to a publisher. If I feel that it's essential to do so before it's submitted to editors, I won't represent the book. And the chances are that an editor won't respond to it, either. When there are obviously "fixable" elements in a manuscript, changes should be made. If the changes aren't made, an editor will think it's sloppy work and reject it.

When a manuscript leaves my office, it has my name on it, too; I am lending it my credibility. I have a relationship with publishers I want to maintain. I want them to take my submissions seriously and to have high regard for the books and authors I represent. If I don't feel that a manuscript is as good as it can be, I won't submit it.

The editorial work that agents may suggest is not as intense as the editorial suggestions an editor might have. Agents are not going to tear the book apart and make you re-structure it; they are not going to go over it paragraph by paragraph. An agent might tell you if a character isn't effective, if motivations aren't clear, if ideas and points are not developed. An agent wants your book to be salable. If it requires major editorial work, the chances are an agent won't take it on.

It may be difficult, at first, to weigh an agent's suggestions reasonably. You want representation, you want an agent sending your book to publishers. But, you don't have to make a decision right away. If an agent calls, ask him to put his ideas and suggestions into a letter so that you can think about them. At the very least, be sure to take careful notes during a phone conversation. If you and a prospective agent can agree editorially, even perhaps with some compromise, your relationship can be effective.

2. *What is the rate of commission?* Most agents work on commission; that is, a percentage of all your earnings from any work the agent sells on your behalf—from a publisher's advance, royalties, sale of reprint rights, or movie, magazine or foreign sales. The rate for literary agents is usually either 10% or 15%. Ten percent used to be standard, but that is changing, and 15% is becoming the norm. It's not that agents are greedier, it is that costs have risen.

What you receive for the commission you pay to your agent is the interest of or dedication of someone whose livelihood is partly dependent on what you produce and how well it sells. An agent's interest in you doesn't stop with the contract. An agent is interested in your career, and what the publisher is going to do to enhance the sales of your book. The agent acts as an intermediary when there are disagreements between you and your publisher, sells subsidiary rights, talks with you about new ideas, reads your proposals and manuscripts, makes suggestions, keeps your name in circulation, thinks of you when editors have ideas for book projects, and consults with you generally about your writing career.

3. *Are there charges beyond a commission?* Will you be charged for Xeroxing, long distance calls, messengers, postage, foreign submissions? All these are reasonable

charges, but you should know what to expect and not be surprised when you receive bills. Some agents will charge for Xeroxing but not for foreign submissions; some will charge for messengers but not for long distance calls.

4. *Are you being asked to sign an Agent/Author Agreement?* Author-agent agreements are not uncommon. Not only do some agents prefer them, some writers do, too. It can make a writer feel more secure knowing that there is a written agreement with his agent. But be careful what you do sign. You don't want to lock yourself into an agreement you may regret later, or may want to terminate for good reason. Some agreements tie an author to an agency indefinitely; some obligate an author to give six months' written notice of a desire to separate; some are for one book, and some for a lifetime's output.

Never sign anything that gives an agency power over your work for an indefinite period of time. Be sure to read the termination clause carefully. If you want to change agents after the first book, you don't want to be held up for several months because you have to give six months' written notice of your intention. And remember, if you do change agents after that first published book, the responsibility for that book remains with the first agent, who will continue to receive all payments from sales and to retain commissions for the lifetime of the contract.

My agency does not, usually, ask an author to sign an agreement with us. However, when we have sold your book and the contract with the publisher is prepared and arrives in our offices, it also includes our agency clause which has become part of the contract. Whether or not you have a signed agreement with your agent, the publisher's contract will include an agency clause. This is the agent's protection. Monies will be paid to you through the agent; the publisher's option to see your next book also gives the agent an option on your next book. Our agency clause below is similar to all agency clauses and is what you will find in the contract for your book if you work through an agent:

The author hereby irrevocably appoints Diane Cleaver, Inc. and Sanford J. Greenburger Associates as his sole and exclusive agent with respect to the said work and authorizes and directs Publisher to make all payments due or to become due to the Author hereunder to and in the name of the said agent, and to accept the receipt of said agent as full evidence and satisfaction of such payments. As sole and exclusive agent, the said agent is authorized to negotiate for the Author throughout the world as to the disposal of all other rights in and to the said work (including without limitation works to which any option herein shall apply). The said agent is further empowered to engage sub-agents for the sale of British Commonwealth and/or translation rights in and to the said work (and the said optioned works) and to pay such sub-agents a commission of up to ten percent (10%) of the money collected from the disposition of any such British Commonwealth and/or translation rights through sub-agents. In consideration for services rendered, the said agent is entitled to receive as its commission fifteen percent (15%) of gross monies paid to the Author hereunder and from all other rights in and to the said work (including the said optioned works), except that such commission shall be reduced to ten percent (10%) as to those monies out of which a sub-agent's commission of five percent (5%) or more is also paid, the said ten percent (10%) to be computed after deduction of the sub-agent's commissions. The provisions of this paragraph shall survive the expiration of this contract.

5. *Where is the agent thinking of submitting your manuscript?* When you ask this question the agent may not yet have decided whether your book should be marketed as a hardcover or a paperback, or which publisher to send it to. There are usually three possibilities: mass market paperback, trade paperback, or hardcover. A mass market paperback—printed and distributed in large numbers—is a rack-size paperback that sells not only through the bookstores but primarily through distribution in supermarkets, drug stores, airports, and similar outlets. A trade paperback is sold primarily through the bookstores, is in a larger format than a mass market title and will have a smaller printing. Both hardcover and mass market paperback publishers often have trade paperback lines.

Where and how a manuscript is submitted depends on what an agent sees as the potential market for the book. You probably have your own ideas about how your book should be published, but don't impose them on the agent. You should discuss the matter, but you shouldn't be adamant about hardcover if the agent believes it has a better chance as a trade paperback or mass market original. The agent knows the market, the editors, and your manuscript. If you insist on one thing and the agent has other ideas, your relationship may suffer. Because you want to be represented, you'll probably go along with the agent on where to submit your manuscript, but you'll resent it, the agent will know it, and you'll both end up—if you persist—with a desultory, unprofitable relationship.

6. *What kinds of authors does the agent generally represent?* You're interested in this not because you want to be represented by somebody with a list of big names, but because you want to know what your agent's interests are and where you fit in. You'll find that most agents represent a wide variety of writers—fiction, nonfiction, serious and popular books. You may not be familiar with the names of the agency's authors, and you may not like all of your agent's books, but it is comforting to know that the agent has a list of clients, that books have sold, that others are coming.

Your relationship with your agent should be a comfortable, trusting, accessible one. You do not have to live in the same town to achieve this. I have relationships with authors I've never met. We conduct our business, and friendship, through correspondence or sometimes on the phone. Even if you live in the same town as your agent, you will find that most of your conversations will be over the phone.

A writer should feel that his agent cares about his work and is doing everything he can to place it with a sympathetic editor and a good publisher for the best price. A writer doesn't want to feel unimportant, or less important than any of the agent's other clients. You should like, trust and respect your agent, and your agent should like and respect you.

Most agents represent dozens of writers. Some are active at the moment, some were more so last year, and others will be next year. During the course of a sale of your manuscript, the relationship you'll have with your agent will be close and more intense. You'll have questions, and your agent will try to answer them. You shouldn't be kept in the dark about decisions; you shouldn't feel railroaded into accepting anything you don't like; and you should feel that comments, offers, and any disagreements are presented to you fairly. The agent is *your* representative and your advisor. Generally, because of your agent's professional experience and knowledge of the marketplace, you will follow his advice. That's what you're paying a commission for.

VIII

SELECTING A PUBLISHER

YOUR AGENT'S RELATIONSHIP with editors, his or her credibility and reputation within the publishing community, are important factors in the selling of your manuscript. Agents do not send manuscripts to publishers in some kind of hit-or-miss method. Selecting the appropriate publisher is an important consideration for the author and the agent.

If your agent lives in New York, the chances are that he or she knows editors in most publishing houses. One of the ways we get to know each other is over lunch, out of the office and off the phone, where there's time to talk more casually about books and the business of books, about authors and new projects. It's a time when editor and agent find out what each of them is interested in. Knowing where an editor comes from, spends his vacations, whether he's married and where he lives can often help my decisions about where to submit certain manuscripts. In spite of all the marketing considerations that always have to be confronted, an editor's decision to buy a manuscript is, first of all, a subjective decision. If an agent knows an editor's interests and concerns, a manuscript might be placed more effectively.

If agents talk to editors regularly, they learn what's happening in the business, who bought what, who is interested in certain areas of publishing, what prices have been paid, what books sound good, what authors look promising, which writers need agents, whether there are ideas around that might be right for a particular author. It's not that agents take notes during these lunches, but they do gain impressions, likings, ideas, information and, over time, a sense of which editors will respond positively to certain books.

When I have a new manuscript to submit, I have to consider the market and ask certain questions:

Who is the audience for this book? I don't know specifically, but I can make a judgment based on whether it's a contemporary women's novel, a serious novel, a humor book, how-to; whether there's anything else like it already out there, the author's reputation in his field of expertise, whether it's a first book, and the author's track record.

Which publishers would reach the right audience? If it's a literary novel or a biography or whatever, I have to think about which publishers have published comparable books in the past and how well they've done with them.

Within those publishing houses, which editors will be most sympathetic and enthusiastic? If I know the editors, I have a sense of what they're interested in and, from what I know of the author, how well they would work together.

Should it be a hardcover, trade, or mass paper? If it's a novel with some potential for serious review attention, I'll choose a hardcover publisher first. If it's suspense or romance or how-to, I might choose mass market paperback. If it's humor or practical or would appeal to a college-age audience, I might go to trade paperback.

What's the competition? This is particularly important in nonfiction areas. I want to know who published books on the same subject, when, how many copies they sold, what is different about the manuscript I'm selling. Is my author an expert, and what does he offer that no one else does?

What is the subsidiary rights potential? Will it be of interest to a foreign market? All books don't travel; many of them are of interest only to American audiences. Are there magazine first serial possibilities, can it be successfully excerpted, and for what magazine? What are book club possibilities—not just Book of the Month Club and the Literary Guild but the History Book Club or the Science Book Club? Are there film possibilities? If it's nonfiction, the chances aren't great; if it's an historical novel with exotic locations, it may be too expensive to produce.

How many copies do I think this book will sell in the general trade? Inevitably, I begin optimistically. I'm representing this book because I believe it's good and that there is a market for it. I also know, however, that the reality of final sales is often disappointing. Most books don't hit the best-seller lists; many books, in fact, sell fewer than 10,000 copies, and many never earn royalties beyond the advance.

How much will I sell this manuscript for? I answer this question, for myself, when I've thought about all the other questions. And I answer with a price range, a low that will be firm and a high that is flexible.

These questions are the questions an editor will ask, too. The answers he will be looking for are: How many copies can we sell? What is the break-even point? Will this book be profitable for the company? I want the answers clear in my own mind for the future discussions I'll be having with editors when I'm negotiating the sale of the book. As a writer, you should consider the same questions. You won't know the answers to all of them, but you can check the publishers' lists and the magazines to get an idea of where your work fits in the market. You should know that you've prepared for the submission as thoroughly as you can, and that there is good reason for publication of your book.

Every manuscript is handled somewhat differently, but basically, there are three ways that agents submit manuscripts: The single submission (one manuscript to one editor); the multiple submission, in which the manuscript goes to several editors (not an acceptable submission procedure for writers themselves to practice, by the way); and an auction, which is handled in the same way as a multiple submission, but differs in that editors interested in buying may bid against one another.

The submission of one manuscript to only one editor at a time is the traditional approach. I do this when I have a specific editor in mind—for any of a variety of reasons—or if it's a novel that might require special attention, or a complex manuscript requiring an editor's expertise. Occasionally, I'll go to only one editor when the market for a particular book might not be large, and there aren't many publishers who would be interested or could publish it well.

The multiple submission—particularly for nonfiction proposals—is most often used by agents. I sent the following letter to eight hardcover publishers with Meg Bogin's book manuscript:

Dear _____,

The Path to Pain Control by Meg Bogin is, I believe, going to be an extraordinarily good book. It's not just a book about pain and how to bear it, it offers a philosophy of chronic pain and how to incorporate it—if you're one of the forty million people who suffer with chronic pain—into your life.

It's not a book about fighting pain; it's not written by a physician or therapist with an empirical point-of-view. It is written by a twenty-nine-year-old woman who lives with chronic pain as the result of a muscle disease. She has thought about her pain and translated what has happened to her body and her mind into a larger philosophy which can help others with chronic pain find their own path to pain control. It is intelligent, accessible and graceful.

Meg Bogin graduated from Sarah Lawrence where she studied Romance Languages and Literature. She has published several articles and translations and received two grants for her work. She has written one book, *The Women Troubadors,* published by Paddington Press and soon to be published by Norton.

I am pleased to enclose her proposal and introduction for *The Path to Pain Control.* I hope you'll like the book as much as I do, and I shall look forward to hearing from you the week ending Friday, September 21st. I am showing this material to several editors.

Best wishes,

In phone conversations with the editors, I made it quite clear that this was not an auction. It was a best-offer situation, which meant publishers could make one offer but would not be told what other publishers offered. When all offers were in, I would accept the best one. Editors understood that they would not be in a bidding situation against other publishers to push the price up. In this type of situation, of course, a considerable amount of trust between the editors and the agent is required. The great advantage of a multiple submission for an agent and author is that with several editors considering the proposal simultaneously, even though they aren't bidding against each other, time does become important and they are competing.

When an editor is interested in the manuscript I've sent, he will call and ask how much money I'm looking for. I'll give the editor a range of what I expect, and remind him that it is a "best-offer" situation and that he has only one chance to make his offer. I also ask when I might expect to receive that offer. The editor will try to find out from me how many other publishers have the manuscript, and whether I have any firm offers yet. I won't tell him precisely how many publishers have the material and certainly not who they are, and I won't give any price information. What I do try to convey is that he is not the only editor interested in this manuscript.

If this is the first call expressing interest in the proposal, I'll then call the other publishers and tell them that I have definite interest from another editor. The other editors will either say they're not interested or ask how much money I'm looking for. I'll tell them what I told the first editor.

When any offers are in—and usually not everyone does make an offer, perhaps two or three—I compare them. The highest advance offer is usually the one you go with, but sometimes if two publishers make the same offer, I'll ask both of them if they can better their offer. They might come back with a little more advance money, but it could be a larger percentage of the royalties for the author or a larger split of subsidiary sales such as reprint/paperback monies to the author's advantage. Whichever publisher makes the best offer, gets the book. If they both stick at the same point the author and I will discuss which publisher we prefer. Perhaps the author has a strong feeling about one of the publishers, perhaps one editor is more enthusiastic than another, perhaps a larger company is better than a smaller one. But at no time do I, as the agent, put the publishers directly in competition with each other, and at all times I tell them the truth as we negotiate toward making a deal.

Multiple submissions—especially of nonfiction book proposals—are popular with agents and writers because the response time from editors is much faster than the single-submission route. It can take weeks for an editor to read a manuscript, whereas a multiple submission usually produces a speedy response: An editor who knows that the proposal has been sent to other publishers, too, doesn't want to lose out on a terrific book because he didn't read a manuscript as fast as another editor did.

I don't always put an expected response date in my submission letter—it depends on the length of the manuscript and its contents—but in my own mind I'm usually giving them three weeks to get back to me. In the second or third week after sending out a multiple submission, I make phone calls to see who's read the manuscript. If an editor hasn't read it yet, my call will prompt him to do so. And then a week later I call again.

Auctions take place all the time but are used sparingly by individual agents. The agent has to be confident that the manuscript he is selling is one that several editors will want. The book has to be big and commercial, or written by a prominent authority in whatever area, or by a celebrity, or be on a topic of immediate or national interest, or it has to be a new book by an author with a profitable track record. An agent does not undertake an auction lightly; there is nothing worse than holding an auction to which no one comes. And it's been known to happen.

The rules of an auction must be clearly defined. In the few auctions I've held, I have not written comprehensive cover letters. Before receiving the manuscript, I call every editor who will be involved and discuss the book and author. This groundwork of talking to editors often takes several weeks and sometimes two or three conversations with each editor. So by the time they receive the manuscript, they're ready for it. My cover letter, which goes out with each manuscript to the publisher (by messenger), simply indicates that this is the manuscript they've been expecting, reminds them of the author's previous publishing record (if noteworthy), and includes a paragraph something like this:

> "First round bids will be evaluated on a comprehensive, best-offer basis, and must be made on or before _____. The book will be auctioned among the top three bidders two days later."

The word "comprehensive" implies that the advance is not the only factor to be considered. I am also interested in royalty splits, paperback reprint splits, advertising, and anything else that looks like a complete offer to me. Of course, the advance is important, but it's only one element I'll be looking at when the top three offers are pitted against each other. The rules of an auction can vary: Some agents ask for written offers, sometimes the bidding takes place without initial best offers. But an auction always means that publishers may bid against each other through the agent conducting that sale.

During the process of selling a manuscript, whether it's by single or multiple submission, or whether it's through an auction, the agent's responsibility is to keep the author informed. All offers are discussed with authors. The agent has a right to negotiate, but not the right to accept an offer without the author's approval. Unless it's an auction, when the agent and author are in pretty constant communication, an agent will usually call the author periodically to bring him up to date on submissions and rejections. If any of the rejections offer useful information, criticism, or advice, agents generally send copies of those letters to the authors. If a writer doesn't hear from the agent every three or four weeks, he should call or write to find out what is happening to his manuscript.

IX

THE DEAL

A SUCCESSFUL NEGOTIATION is one in which both the buyer and the seller feel that they've made a good, fair deal. An agent and author should feel that they have received the best advance and the best contractual terms possible within the framework of the negotiation. The publisher should believe that he has bought a book within the framework of what seems profitable and reasonable. No one should leave the negotiation thinking that he's been pushed to the wall or cheated.

Sometimes, if two or three publishers are interested in the same manuscript, an agent will receive widely divergent offers. In spite of all the market analysis that goes into deciding how large an advance is reasonable—and the same kind of analysis is done by publishers when they make an offer—there are often different views about the value of any given manuscript. Some publishers will decide not to make an offer; others will make offers that can range from $2,500 to $60,000, or $200,000 to $850,000. This is especially true in the case of unknown authors with no track record, who come out of the blue with a book that seems suddenly very salable. There is no predetermined or fixed price value on manuscripts. It depends on the state of the economy, what about this book is new or original, or compelling, or a breakthrough idea. It also depends on the belief and enthusiasm of an agent, an editor, a publisher and a sales department. And these are elements you can't always pin down. It's also why offers can'range so widely and why no two submissions or negotiations are ever the same.

As an experienced agent, I can tell you what I am going to do, what I think about your book, what I expect to happen, what the alternatives are, but I can't guarantee that any of it will happen in the way that I might anticipate. Within the negotiation itself, however, I can be flexible enough to take advantage of information an editor might give me, or I can ignore other information that might not be to my advantage.

During the process of negotiation, agents and editors give each other as little information as possible. I won't reveal to an editor exactly how much interest I have had from other publishers, or who they are, or even if any other publisher has expressed interest. I don't want to give an editor my bottom-line figure or to let him know how far I can be pushed. And editors approach the negotiations the same way. They won't tell me how high their offer can go—they always come in lower than their top figure. Once the negotiation begins, they won't tell me how much they want the book.

I have the kind of voice that tells a listener who knows me exactly what I'm feeling—whether I'm in a good mood or depressed or bored or excited. During negotiations I consciously make every effort to keep my voice very cool and unemotional. I don't want to tell an editor how much I want this deal to work out, I don't want him to know that he's my best bet or that he's with the publisher I want, or that I'd rather be with someone else, or that we would take a lower advance. My position is that if the editor wants the manuscript, he's the one who will have to make a good, strong offer because he believes I have alternatives.

Editors sometimes make pre-emptive offers—that is, offers they hope will be high enough for me to accept, thereby eliminating any competition from other publishers. The manuscript has gone to several editors. Within a few days, a call comes in from one of those editors. He would like to make a pre-emptive offer. Am I interested?

As I listen to the editor, I try to decide whether I want to hear the offer and how much it has to be for me to accept. If this publisher is keen, won't others be equally eager? The answer is no, not always. I have an estimate of the book's worth in my head. Unless there's a good reason not to—if I have other very strong expressions of interest—I will ask the editor what he is offering. I listen carefully, say thank you, and hang up.

In any negotiation, you do not make a decision before you've had time to think about it. Usually a publisher will give you twenty-four hours to respond to his pre-emptive offer.

If the offer is around the figure I had in mind, or higher, I will be inclined to accept it. If it's too low, I will say no. Before calling the publisher back, however, I talk it over with the author. Generally, when a writer hears of a pre-emptive offer, he is put in something of a dilemma with the thought that if one publisher wants it so much, maybe he'll get more from another publisher. To weigh this, we'll consider who else has the book, what kind of responses we've had, what we're still likely to get, what the publisher knows that we don't, why he made a pre-emptive offer, and finally we'll make a decision to accept it or not.

Agreement is reached when the advance offered and the terms of the contract are satisfactory to us—to the author and to the publisher. Prior to publication, the publisher pays the author an advance against future royalties. If the publisher is buying a complete manuscript and no more work is required, it is traditional for the advance to be paid in one full payment. More often, manuscripts are only partially complete or need further work at the time agreement is reached. In that case, it is customary for the publisher to pay half on signing of the contract and half on final acceptance of the manuscript. But all this depends on the amount of the advance, whether the book is to be hardcover, softcover or both. The advance can be split into two payments or three or four, stretching out from signing to publication and sometimes to several months beyond. Usually the payment schedule is negotiated before final agreement on the contract is reached.

For the advance paid to an author, the publisher is buying certain rights, and these rights are also negotiable. To reach the initial stages of agreement where you can say, we have a deal, the major issues are royalties, U.S. or world rights, possible paperback splits and first serial rights. A deal is made (usually over the phone) between an editor and agent when these major issues have been discussed, an offer incorporating those items made, and the offer accepted. There are dozens of clauses in any publisher's contract, all of them open to negotiations, but many of these are more often discussed after agreement on the basic contract is reached.

It isn't that publishers are unreasonable or unfair to authors—at least not most of the time—but they are naturally negotiating in their own interests and not the author's. An agent is working on the writer's behalf.

X

SUBSIDIARY RIGHTS

SELLING BOOK PUBLICATION rights to a publisher is only one element of the financial rewards that may be generated by your manuscript. Subsidiary, or secondary, rights are a source of profit and publicity for the book, for the publisher and for the author. Once the advance has been agreed upon for the sale of book rights, the major clauses of a contract of concern to the author are book club, reprint, first and second serialization, foreign and film rights.

If you don't have an agent, the sale of these rights will be handled by the publisher. Most publishers have active subsidiary rights departments who arrange these sales. If you do have an agent, it is usually to your advantage to have subsidiary rights handled by your agent, not because your agent has better connections than the publisher, but because the money earned from the sale of the rights you have not granted to the publisher will flow directly to you. If the publisher handles subsidiary sales on your behalf, the earnings are applied against your advance. If, for example, you sold your manuscript to a publisher for an advance of

$7,500 and the publisher sold a chapter or an excerpt to a magazine for $1,000 before publication of the book, that money will be applied against your advance, so that now you "owe" the publisher only $6,500. Until that advance of $7,500 is earned back through bookstore sales or subsidiary sales, you will not receive additional royalties from your publisher. If your agent made the same sale, *you* would immediately receive what the magazine paid minus the agent's commission.

If you don't have an agent, you will, when you accept the publisher's advance offer, be selling him the subsidiary rights. And there's no way to avoid this, since you don't have the connections and know-how to sell these rights yourself, and you won't want to lose out on possible income. Also, some magazines won't accept submissions directly from authors, and it's virtually impossible to get a Hollywood studio or producer to consider your work without an agent or a publisher.

Motion picture studios are nervous about possible lawsuits that may result from authors who claim that films produced at some later date have some similarity to manuscripts they submitted—even though many people could be working on the same idea at the same time. It's the way the idea is used and presented that is ultimately important. Producers and studios guard against possible legal action by working only through publishers and agents.

Most publishers work very hard to sell every subsidiary right they control. It's to their advantage to do so, since, in effect, they earn a commission for the sales they make, and it adds to the overall profits they realize from the book.

The following subsidiary rights are traditionally held by publishers whether there's an agent or not:

Book Clubs

Not all books are suitable for book clubs, but many are, and your publisher will offer your manuscript to the club or clubs that seem most appropriate and likely to take it as a selection. If a book is taken by a club, an advance against the number of copies the club expects to sell to their members is paid to the publisher. Your publisher will retain 50% of those monies, and 50% will be credited to your royalty account.

There are two major general-interest book clubs: The Literary Guild and The Book-of-the-Month Club (BOMC), but there are also other smaller general-interest clubs, and dozens of clubs that specialize in cooking or science or crafts, mysteries, history, family life, or architecture, and many other areas. If a book is a Main Selection of one of the major clubs—especially if book clubs have bid against each other for the rights—there is considerable profit to be made; $80,000/$100,000 and sometimes more is not uncommon. Most books are not Main Selections, and while the financial rewards are therefore more modest—$4,000/$10,000 perhaps—the value of additional publicity and thousands of readers is substantial.

Because of the additional sales and money they generate, book clubs have always been important to publishers, but in recent years they've assumed a new prominence. Publishers make submissions to book clubs several months before publication—usually when a promising manuscript goes into production. By the time the club sees the manuscript, it will often know the extent of the publisher's commitment to that book, what the first printing might be, what advertising monies will be available, whether it has sales potential to be a big commercial book, and whether it is likely to receive good critical attention.

The Literary Guild and the BOMC receive between 100 and 150 manuscripts and galleys every week. First readings are done by "readers." The Literary Guild has in-house staff readers who make recommendations to senior editors, who in turn make recommendations to editorial directors. For first readings, the BOMC uses outside free-lance readers with expertise in various fields. Depending on that first report, the manuscript is either rejected or read by an in-house reader. If it gets enough positive readings, it will become an "A" book, that is, a book to be considered by its panel of judges as a Main Selection.

Apart from the possible financial rewards of a book club sale, there is the added bonus of its effect on the publisher. Having a book selected by a book club is usually the first outside confirmation your publisher receives that he made the right decision in taking on a book. If a publisher has been half-hearted about the possibilities of a particular book, a club sale can turn his thinking around and increase the potential sale with an increased first printing and possibly more advertising. It's ammunition publishers can use when they sell the book to the stores and in other subsidiary sales. It doesn't have to be a big book club sale; even a modest book club commitment helps.

Reprint Rights

These rights are traditionally retained by publishers. Although it fluctuates, the reprint market has shrunk in recent years, and there is less money to be made from reprint sales. Prices paid to hardcover publishers by paperback companies for reprint rights vary partly because of the state of the economy, but also because paperback companies are now more interested in publishing their own original titles. They often compete with hardcover houses for the same authors. There are also fewer paperback companies for hardcover houses to sell to. In the last few years, Ballantine Books has absorbed Fawcett; Berkley has absorbed Jove; Berkley/Jove has absorbed Playboy and Ace. It wasn't so long ago that almost all hardcover books went into reprint, and for many of those books, large amounts of money were paid. Today fewer hardcover books have reprint sales, and in general the money paid is less. There still are, of course, the six-figure reprint sales (and a few even in seven figures), but they're less frequent than they were a few years ago.

In general, a book is sold for reprint through an auction. Auctions are conducted by the original hardcover publisher's subsidiary rights department. They are not feasible for authors to manage. Copies of a manuscript, galleys, or the finished book are sent to paperback houses with all the sales and background data—book club sale, film sale, first printing, advertising budget—and if the book has been published, reviews and comments. The auction is truly operative only with the big books or name authors. Most often, a paperback house will call up and make an offer, the hardcover house will call around and check to see if anyone else wants to offer, and if not, will accept that first offer. And frequently it's low. Because it's now a buyer's market for reprint houses, they can often make modest offers of $3,000 and $5,000 and have them accepted. The feeling on the part of the agent and original publisher is that, while it may not be a strong offer, it's better to keep the book in print in a paperback edition than not at all.

Second Serial Rights
These rights refer to magazine or newspaper publication of a book or parts of it after publication. These rights are also handled by the publisher. The money paid is usually modest, but if a chapter, condensation or excerpt runs close enough to the publication date of the book, the publicity value can be very high and stimulate further sales of the book. In addition to a small excerpt or chapter sale to a magazine or newspaper, there is the possibility of newspaper syndication through such syndicates as The New York Times Syndicate, Field Enterprises or The Chicago Tribune. With syndication, a segment of a book will appear not only in one newspaper but in several across the country.

The following rights are traditionally retained by the agent on behalf of the author:

First Serialization
Unless negotiated otherwise, First Serial rights are retained by the author and sold by his or her agent. First serial means sales to magazines or newspapers before publication. Usually, the payment for first serial rights is higher than for the second serial, and such a sale can build early interest in your forthcoming book.

Foreign Rights
Many books by American authors sell in foreign markets, and while the advances are lower, it is an additional source of income.

Most agents sell the work of the authors they represent through sub-agents located in other countries. Many large foreign publishers also retain literary scouts based in the United States—people who literally do scout the American market for books that might be of interest to their markets.

If we think a book will "travel" well (and not all books do), our agency sends copies of that book to our sub-agents. We rarely send a manuscript—foreign publishers prefer the finished book—unless it's by an author they've previously published. Also, by then we have additional information—how many copies have been printed, whether it's selling well—and can send reviews and information about serial sales, book club and reprint.

Often, books that sell well in the United States don't sell abroad because they've been written for an American audience and deal with things that are of specific appeal here. Different countries have different specialized interests, too. It's hard to generalize, but France and Sweden seem to like suspense, Italy likes romance, Britain likes some of our serious fiction, and the Japanese buy a lot of our nonfiction.

Film Rights

These rights will be handled by your agent if you have one. Agents, like publishers, often work with West Coast film agents as sub-agents when they sell movie rights. Whether I use a West Coast agent or not depends on the book. As in every other aspect of publishing, everyone's first interest is in the "big" book. Hollywood agents will often reject a book if it's not commercial enough. When I consider film rights sales for a book, I think about whether I have the right connections to sell it myself, or whether I might be more effective if I work with a West Coast agent.

As soon as a book is scheduled by a publisher, it begins to appear on subsidiary rights department lists. Many studios and producers have "story editors" whose job it is to find out about future books that might be of interest to them. Long before a book is published, I start to get calls from story editors at studios asking to see the manuscript. Having a manuscript read or "covered" by a film company is never a problem; the problem is finding the person with the right vision and enthusiasm, who will see the possibilities of making the book into a film.

There are few major studios left, but there are dozens, if not hundreds, of independent film producers who have arrangements with the studios or have the ability to find backing for their productions. Most films are actually made by the independents, who in turn have distribution set-ups or arrangements with the studios.

A producer often gets his first information about a new work through a report from a story editor, and producers are very competitive about getting the first look or an exclusive look at a manuscript. A manuscript can find its way to a producer through the production department or even the mail room of your publisher, and it can be covered and rejected with no control from the agent or the publisher. Hollywood covers everything, but of the "everything" they cover, very few options are taken, and even fewer films are ultimately made.

Of course, movies are made, and some of them are from books. When I get inquiries from story editors or producers about a book they know I represent, it's often a long time till publication, and I don't have a manuscript to show them. By the time I have a final copy of the manuscript, I've usually collected the names of several film people who want to see it. Unless it's really a best seller (for which I might conduct an auction), I usually let everyone who has asked read the manuscript. Most times the manuscript is returned, but if someone is interested in the script possibilities of a book, they offer an option: perhaps $5,000 for a one-year option against a buy-out price that might be $100,000 or $150,000 for a feature film and half that if it becomes a television movie. Many options are for much less than $5,000. The producer will try to option a book for as little as possible. What he or she is interested in during that year's option period is in seeing whether it's possible to make a film, whether anyone else is interested in the idea. Producers need backers, so when they take an option they usually have an idea of which studio will be interested. They are also thinking about the book in terms of the film, the star, the scriptwriter, the director. If those things come together, they will commit themselves to producing a film from the book. Without a star or a name director, it's often hard to get the right backing. Very few books are bought outright, that is, paying $100,000 or whatever the buy-out price may be on signing of the agreements. Even when a book is bought outright it often doesn't get made into a movie. For example, Gay Talese's book, *Thy Neighbor's Wife* sold for two million dollars to United Artists. William Friedkin, the director, was under contract to them and wanted to make the film. Friedkin *(Rosemary's Baby, Cruising, The Shining)* was important to United Artists so they put up the money. But, Friedkin changed his mind, and the movie still hasn't been made and might never be.

When a book sells to Hollywood an author is selling all rights to its content and has no control over the film, its content or the way it's presented. The film is the director's vision, not the author's. The director is buying an idea, an ambience, a plot, and all of it is open to his cinematic interpretation. What happens in a book is not necessarily what the audience will see on film. Books and films are different mediums, and it can be a painful experience for the author of a novel when he sees his work on film to find that it's different from his book.

XI

CONTRACTS

AGREEMENT made this _____ day of _____, 198_
between (Publisher's Name) and (Author's Name)
hereinafter called "Author" being the Author and Proprietor of a work at present entitled:

_____

Title

All publishers have a basic contract called the boiler-
plate, all of which contain essentially the same clauses.
The language varies from contract to contract, some
are more detailed than others, and the order of the
clauses might be different in different contracts. But
basically they all spell out what rights you are selling
the publisher and what the publisher's responsibility is
in publishing your book.

Contracts are confusing on first reading. They discuss things an author may never have considered or
heard of before. Even now, after several years as an
agent, I still from time to time come across a clause that
I don't understand or that is so vague that it can be
interpreted in different ways. Some things are negoti-

able and some are not; it often depends on the impor-
tance of the author and his previous record. If you're
an author not represented by an agent, it's sometimes
difficult to negotiate very much on your first contract,
but as you continue to write more books you will, in all
probability, be able to gain some concessions from your
publisher. Negotiation is partly a matter of skill, but it's
also an ability to stop when something doesn't quite
make sense or doesn't sound entirely fair. Rather than
just ignoring whatever it is, you begin to question in-
consistencies. Never worry that you don't know
enough or that you'll sound silly if you ask. You should
understand your contract, and you should ask the
questions that puzzle you.

RIGHTS GRANTED
Author grants to Publisher for the full term of copyright available in
each country included within the territory covered by this Agreement,
including renewals and extensions, under any copyright laws now or
hereafter in force the sole and exclusive right to print, publish, copy,
and vend the work and the other rights hereinafter referred to on the
terms set forth, throughout the world or sometimes only the United
States and Canada.

This clause usually appears at the beginning of a
contract. It states that you, the author, are granting the
publisher the right to print and publish your book.
"Territory" indicates the specific areas of the world
that right covers. If you don't have an agent, you will
usually be selling World Rights to the publisher, which
would give him the right to sell your book to foreign
publishers. If you do have an agent, you will perhaps
give the publisher only the right to publish your book
in the United States and Canada. You would thus re-

tain British and translation rights, which your agent would sell on your behalf.

Even if you do have an agent, publishers may ask for World Rights. Foreign sales can mean additional income for the publisher, and so defray his initial investment. This is especially true of illustrated books with high production costs. If your publisher makes early sales to foreign publishers (that is, well before publication in the United States), he can reduce his press costs by printing several thousand additional copies of your book for the foreign publishers along with his own print run. The more copies, the less expensive each copy of the book is.

Whether to offer a publisher World Rights or not is also a point of negotiation which can be advantageous to an author. If, for example, an author needs or wants an advance of $10,000 to complete the work on his manuscript, and the publisher offers only $8,500, an agent can suggest to the publisher that they handle foreign rights for an additional $1,500 advance. That would give the author an advance of $10,000. The publisher, for his part, and the agent, on behalf of the author, will try to figure out whether there is any advantage (as publisher) in buying or (as agent) in selling these rights.

·PUBLICATION
 Publisher shall publish the work at its own expense, in the style and manner and at the price which it shall deem best suited to its sale and under such original imprint as it deems advisable.

This clause points out that you, the author, have no right to control the way your book looks. It is also an open-ended clause that doesn't state when the publisher will actually publish your book; it could be next year or in ten years. As agent, I always insist on including a time limitation. After "Publisher shall publish the work . . ." I would insert: "within twenty-four months of acceptance of the Work." If there isn't a time limitation in your contract initially, you should try to have one inserted. It might not be two years, it could be one year or three. The point is not to let your manuscript languish indefinitely. It's rare that this happens, but it can, and sometimes does, if a time limitation isn't included.

You will see that the last phrase of this clause states that the publisher may publish your book "under such original imprint as it deems advisable." Many publishers have more than one imprint. Doubleday, for example, has the Doubleday imprint, Anchor Books, Dolphin Books, and The Crime Club. However, when a book is sold, you will be told how a publisher intends to publish it and under what imprint.

MANUSCRIPT: CHARACTER, DUE DATE, AUTHOR'S ALTERATIONS

(a) Author shall deliver to Publisher two (2) finally revised copies of the work, satisfactory to Publisher in content and form, including all illustrations and other graphic material essential to the work, in a form ready for reproduction, not later than_____.
If Author delivers only one (1) finally revised copy of the work or if the second copy is not clean or legible, Publisher may have the original manuscript duplicated and the expense charged to Author's royalty account.

(b) Author shall also deliver to Publisher an index, if required by Publisher, promptly after proof is available for making the index. If Author fails to supply all such index, illustrations, and other graphic material in a form ready for reproduction, Publisher may obtain it and charge the expense thereof against Author's earnings hereunder. It is understood that such material is considered a part of the work and that all rights granted and warranties and indemnities made to Publisher hereunder apply also to use of such material.

(c) If Author incorporates into the work any material previously published and not in the public domain, he shall procure at his expense written authorization satisfactory to Publisher to publish it in the work and shall deliver copies of such authorization to Publisher with the manuscript.

(d) The provisions of subparagraphs (a) and (b) hereof as to the character, condition, and time of receipt of the copies of the work are of the essence of the Agreement, and in the event of Author's default hereunder Publisher may, at its option, any time prior to actual publication of the work, terminate this Agreement without prejudice to any other remedy.

(e) Expense of Author's proof corrections exceeding ten per cent (10%) of cost of composition shall be charged against Author's earnings hereunder.

(f) Any sums paid to Author as advance royalties or otherwise shall be returned to Publisher on demand if said copies are not delivered as provided in subparagraph (a) hereof.

(g) Author represents that he has retained a copy of the manuscript and the Publisher shall not be liable for any loss resulting to Author from a destruction or other loss of the copies delivered to Publisher unless Publisher shall have failed to carry appropriate insurance therefore, if the same is available and has been requested in writing by Author and at Author's expense.

This clause states not only the date upon which you agree to deliver your manuscript in final form to the publisher, but also exactly what is meant by "manuscript" and what you are responsible for: delivery of two copies of the text, providing the index, if one is needed (this is actually done during page proof stage, after page numbers—folios—are inserted by the printer. The author may do the index, or the publisher will hire an indexer to do it and then charge the author for that expense). The author will also be charged the costs for permissions, if the manuscript includes copyrighted work.

Also note the final subclause. The author is entirely

responsible for his or her manuscript. It is not the publisher's responsibility if it is lost or destroyed. *Never, never, never* give *anyone*—agent, publisher, friend or relative—your only copy of a manuscript. Always keep one copy in a safe place.

ADVANCE ROYALTY
    Publisher shall pay to Author, or his duly authorized representative, the following advance which shall be charged against Author's earnings under this Agreement:

An advance, whether it's $1,500 or $150,000, is an advance payment against future royalties earned from the sale of your book. Before you receive further royalty checks, the royalties earned from the sale of your book will go toward paying back the publisher's advance to you. The advance is, in effect, in anticipation of sales, showing the good faith of the publisher and his confidence in your book. Not all books earn back their advances; that is the publisher's risk, not yours, and if royalties do not even equal the advance, the author keeps the money received prior to publication.

TRADE ROYALTY IN THE UNITED STATES
    Publisher shall pay to Author:
    (a) On all copies, less returns, of the regular trade edition sold by Publisher in the United States of America (except as hereinafter set forth), the following royalties based on the retail price:

Trade royalties are monies paid by the publisher to the author from sales of books to the trade—that is through bookstores. The standard royalty on hardcover books is 10% of the retail price of a book on the sale of the first 5,000 copies; 12½% on the next 5,000 copies sold, and 15% on all copies sold thereafter.

Sometimes a publisher will ask that 10% extend to the first 7,500 copies rather than 5,000. This is especially true of first novels or specialized books when the market is not established or the book is very costly to produce or has expensive illustrations. Going to a 12½% royalty too soon can sometimes mean the difference, to a publisher, of breaking even or taking a financial loss. This, of course, is the publisher's argument. As an agent I try to resist it.

Standard royalties on original mass market (sold by newsstands or supermarkets, as well as in bookstores) paperbacks usually begin at 6%. If it's an author's first book, it might be difficult to reach a higher royalty, but it's reasonable to expect a break at, say, 100,000 or 150,000 copies, to an 8% royalty. Although the royalties on mass paperback are lower than hardcover, the print numbers are very different, too. A hardcover might have an initial print run of 7,500 copies; it is not unusual for a mass market paperback to have an initial print run of 75,000 or even 100,000 copies.

Royalties on trade paperbacks (larger format than mass market and more expensive cover prices) begin at either 6% or 7½%. Often where the royalty scale begins depends on the author's sales record. Sometimes it is possible to negotiate a royalty break to 10% after sales of 30,000 or 50,000 copies, but it's often a battle. Trade paperbacks are printed in smaller numbers than mass market; often an initial print run will be 10,000 to 15,000 copies, and the publisher's break-even point is higher than on mass market books, which have a larger print run. While the royalty rates on trade and mass market paperbacks appear comparable, it's harder for both the publisher and the author to realize the same financial return on trade paperbacks as they can from mass market sales. Trade paperbacks are more expensive to produce, and the retail price is lower than for a hardcover book, so the publisher will fight to keep the royalty schedule low.

CANADIAN ROYALTY
On all copies of the regular trade edition of the work sold in the Dominion of Canada, an amount equal to five per cent (5%) of the United States of America retail price.

OTHER EXPORT MARKETS
On all copies of the regular trade edition of the work sold by Publisher to other export markets, an amount equal to eight per cent (8%) of the United States of America retail price.

Because of government restrictions, tariffs and the fact that the Canadian dollar is worth considerably less than the U.S. dollar, royalties earned from the sale of your book in Canada are lower. Other export markets are called the "open market," meaning that the original United States edition of a book may be shipped to and sold in other countries, and the publisher is not restrained by contract from selling it in those foreign markets.

SPECIAL SALES
On all copies of the regular trade edition of the work sold through Publisher's Special Sales Department, as distinct from sales made to bookstores or jobbers, five per cent (5%) of the retail price, except as hereinafter provided.

Special sales include such selling devices as mail order and premium sales. In "mail order," a coupon is placed in newspapers and magazine ads for a book that can be ordered by mail. It's an effective way of selling *some* books, usually for the publisher's more expensive books. Costs for the advertising, mailing and staff needed to handle mail order books are high, making it unprofitable for the publisher to pay regular royalties. Mail order is used sparingly by publishers, but if a book has a high retail price, if it's selling well in the general trade, and if it's a practical or special audience book, mail order can be effective and profitable.

Premium sales are bulk sales, usually to an organization or company that can use a book to promote their own product or service. For example, banks might buy copies of a financial planning book to give out to new customers; a seed company might promote sales of its garden products by offering a gardening book as a premium. Because the company or organization is usually buying two or three thousand books, they are given a special discount, hence the author receives lower royalties.

ANNUAL PAYMENT LIMITATION
   Notwithstanding anything to the contrary in this Agreement, Publisher shall in no event pay to Author out of the sums accruing to Author more than ($) during any one calendar year. In the event the sums to Author's credit exceed such annual maximum payment, such excess shall be retained by Publisher in its general funds and shall be paid by it to Author in successive calendar years provided each yearly payment shall not exceed the maximum herein stated.

If your book is a huge success and you will be receiving large royalty checks, you may not, for tax purposes, want to be paid all your earnings in any one year. If you are earning so much money, however, you may be better off to take your royalty earnings when they're due and invest them. If you don't, your publisher will be earning interest on the monies he's hold-

ing on your behalf. If you find yourself in this situation, you should definitely consult a tax accountant
and lawyer. You do not have to complete this clause by
adding a limitation figure.

PUBLISHING RIGHTS OUTSIDE THE UNITED STATES and
TRANSLATIONS
Author grants to Publisher the sole and exclusive right to sell English
language and translation rights in and to the work in book or serial form
(in full-length, condensed, or abridged versions) for publication in
countries other than the United States, for publication in the territory
specified in Paragraph 1(a). Publisher shall pay to Author seventy-five
per cent (75%) of the net proceeds of such sale.

If you have an agent, this clause, unless negotiated
otherwise, will be eliminated from the contract. Not all
publishers retain 25% of such proceeds; some retain
20% or even 10%. This probably isn't very negotiable
on a first-book contract, however, but it might well be
on second and third books.

BOOK CLUBS
Author grants to Publisher the sole and exclusive right to license the
right to print, publish, and sell an edition of the work to a book club,
including any book club owned or operated by a subsidiary or affiliate of
Publisher, or to any organization which operates on the basis of plate
rental or purchase of book club rights (in full-length, condensed, or
abridged versions). Publisher shall pay to Author fifty per cent (50%) of
the net proceeds of such licenses received by Publisher.

It is traditional for the publisher to retain and sell
book club rights. The split is 50% to the publisher and
50% to the author. This isn't negotiable.

REPRINT
Author grants to Publisher the sole and exclusive right to sell to
other publishers, including any subsidiary or affiliate or division of Publisher, the right to bring out a reprint edition of the work (in full-length,
condensed, or abridged versions), which sale shall provide that such

reprints shall not appear on the market within one year after the publication date of trade publication. Publisher shall pay to Author fifty per cent (50%) of the proceeds of such sales, except that in the case of such a sale to Publisher's reprint division, Publisher shall pay to Author one-half the amount which the reprint division shall credit to Publisher. In the event that a reprint edition of the work is published and sold by any subsidiary or affiliate or a division of Publisher, the license to publish the work will, to the extent possible, be on terms similar to the terms of current agreements for similar licenses between Publisher and an unrelated reprint publisher.

The right to sell a reprint edition of your book is traditionally held by the publisher. Reprint nearly always means hardcover to paperback. In a contract for a paperback original, you will see a similar clause that covers the possibility that the paperback publisher may decide either to publish a hardcover edition of your book themselves or to offer the right to do so to another publisher. They might do this because (a) they feel there's a large enough hardcover market to justify such publication, (b) because they see the possibility of wide review attention, or (c) because they want to be your primary publisher and control all the publishing rights. The standard reprint split is 50% to the publisher and 50% to the author. However, this is often negotiable, especially for authors who have published previous books. A publisher may agree to a 60/40 split in the author's favor, if the book sells for over a specific amount of money. For example, they may agree to 50/50 if reprint rights bring $100,000, and 60/40 on all monies above that figure.

FIRST SERIAL

Author grants to Publisher the sole and exclusive right to sell, in the territory specified in Paragraph 1, the work or parts of it for publication in serial form in newspapers or periodicals and excerpts from the work for publication in newspapers or periodicals before publication in book form. Publisher shall pay to Author ninety per cent (90%) of the net proceeds of such sales (except on sales for serial publication in countries other than the United States under Paragraph 6 hereof).

If you have an agent this clause will be eliminated from the contract unless otherwise negotiated, and these sales will be handled by him. If you don't have an agent, the publisher will act as your agent in placing a chapter or excerpt with magazines and newspapers.

SECOND SERIAL
Author grants to Publisher the sole and exclusive right to sell, in the territory specified in Paragraph 1, the work or parts of it for publication in serial form in newspapers or periodicals and excerpts from the work for publication in newspapers or periodicals after publication in book form (provided such rights have not been retained by the purchaser of the first serial rights). Publisher shall pay to Author fifty per cent (50%) of the net proceeds of such sales (except on sales for serial publications in countries other than the United States under Paragraph 6 hereof).

Second serial sales occur *after* book publication, and the publisher retains these rights. The 50/50 split on earnings is not negotiable.

PERMISSIONS, EXTRACTS, ANTHOLOGIES,
ABRIDGED VERSIONS
(a) Author grants to Publisher, in the territory specified in Paragraph 1 hereof, after publication of the work in book form, the right (1) to license for publication an adaptation of all or part of the work, and (2) to sell the work or extracts therefrom for use in periodicals or books (provided such rights have not been retained by the purchasers of the first serial rights), but not in its entirety in book form except as provided in Paragraphs 6, 7, and 8. Publisher shall pay to Author fifty per cent (50%) of the proceeds of such sales (except on sales in countries other than the United States under Paragraph 6 hereof).
(b) No payment shall be made to Author by Publisher for permission gratuitously given by Publisher, before or after publication of the work in book form, to publish extracts from the work to benefit the sale thereof.

When a book stays in print over a period of years, it may become source material for other writers and permissions for such use can bring in additional monies. The publisher usually handles this.

MOTION PICTURES, DRAMATIZATION
PUBLIC READINGS

Author grants Publisher the sole and exclusive right to sell motion picture rights, dramatic rights with or without music, public reading and other non-dramatic performing rights throughout the world in and to and in connection with the said work. Publisher shall pay to Author ninety per cent (90%) of the proceeds of such sales, except sound recording (see Paragraph 16). Any sales of motion picture rights to the work may grant to the purchaser the right to publish, for advertising and exploitation, excerpts, summaries, and synopses of the work or dramatizations or motion pictures thereof, but no such excerpts, summaries or synopses shall exceed 7500 words in length, nor shall they appear as having been written by Author, nor shall they be offered to any person, firm, or corporation for a monetary consideration.

RADIO AND TELEVISION

Author grants to Publisher the sole and exclusive right to sell radio and/or television rights, throughout the world, in and to and in connection with said work. Publisher shall pay to Author ninety per cent (90%) of the proceeds of such sales.

If you have an agent, you will retain these rights, and the clause will be cut from the contract; if you don't have an agent your publisher will handle these rights.

USE BY NON-PROFIT ORGANIZATIONS

Publisher is authorized to grant permission, at no charge and without paying royalty to Author, for use of the work by recognized non-profit organizations for the physically disabled, such as, but not limited to, the right to put the work into Braille or talking books.

It is standard to grant these rights without charge.

SEMI-ANNUAL ACCOUNTING

(a) Publisher shall render statements of sales semi-annually as of

April thirtieth and October thirty-first and make payment of monies due within four months thereafter. If the work has not earned the amount of royalties advanced or Author has received an overpayment of royalties or is otherwise indebted to Publisher, Publisher may deduct the same from any sum due or to become due Author under this Agreement.

(b) Publisher may, for the first three periods following publication, set up a reserve of fifteen per cent (15%) of the earnings due Author, to provide for returns.

(c) Publisher shall, on the written request of Author, cause the public accountants regularly employed by Publisher to furnish to Author a certified copy of his latest semi-annual royalty statement.

Reports on sales and earnings of books are usually made twice a year. You will receive a royalty statement from your publisher and, if there is a profit, a check for additional royalties earned. It is also usual for publishers to hold back some monies against return of unsold books. The 15% stated in this clause is modest. The reserve held by some publishers can go as high as 40% on the first accounting period. Some contracts don't tell you what percentage of earnings and for how long a reserve against returns will be held. It can be difficult to pin a publisher down, but it is worth negotiating for some limitations on the percentage of monies a publisher may hold in reserve.

AUTHOR'S COPIES

Publisher shall furnish to Author, free of charge, ten copies of the regular trade edition of the work as published; and should Author desire any more copies for personal use, they shall be supplied at one-half the retail price. Copies thus purchased shall not be resold. Author will be billed for these copies and payment shall be made within thirty (30) days of receipt of bill unless Publisher wishes to charge this amount to Author's royalty account, provided said account has excess royalties accrued over and above the advance royalty paid to Author.

You will see from this clause that authors do not receive an endless supply of their own books. Most standard contracts state that authors shall receive ten free copies, but it is possible to negotiate for fifteen or twenty copies.

WARRANTY

Author represents and warrants to Publisher that:

(a) The work is original.

(b) He is the sole author and proprietor thereof, and has full power to enter into this Agreement.

(c) The work is not in the public domain, has never before been published in whole or in part in any form and he has not entered into or become subject to any contract, agreement, or understanding with respect thereto other than this Agreement.

(d) If published, this work will not infringe upon any proprietary right at common law, or any statutory copyright, or any other right whatsoever.

(e) The work is innocent, and contains no matter whatsoever that is obscene, libelous, in violation of any right of privacy, or otherwise in contravention of law.

INDEMNITY

(a) Author shall indemnify and hold Publisher harmless from any claim, suit, or action, and any expense or damage in consequence thereof, asserted by reason of Publisher's exercise or enjoyment of any of its rights hereunder or by reason of any warranty or indemnity made by Publisher in connection with the exercise of any such rights, as provided in subparagraphs (b), (c), (d), and (e) hereof.

(b) Publisher shall have the right to defend such claim, suit, or action by counsel of its selection and with the consent of Author to settle the same on such terms as it deems advisable.

(c) In the event a final judgment is entered against Publisher, Author shall be liable for and shall pay to Publisher the amount of said judgment and shall reimburse Publisher for any and all expenses incurred in said action, including counsel fees.

(d) In the event of a settlement, Author shall be liable for and pay to Publisher (1) fifty per cent (50%) of the amounts paid by Publisher in settlement and (2) fifty per cent (50%) of the amounts paid by Publisher for counsel fees and other expenses.

(e) In the event such claim, suit, or action is discontinued or dismissed without liability to Publisher, Author shall be liable for and shall pay to Publisher fifty per cent (50%) of the amounts paid by Publisher for counsel fees and other expenses.

(f) Publisher shall have the further right to withhold and apply any royalties or other sums due Author under this or any other agreement as security for Author's obligation under this Paragraph 22.

(g) The warranties contained in Paragraph 21 and the indemnities contained in this Paragraph 22 shall survive the termination of this Agreement.

Publisher shall have the right in its discretion to extend the benefit of Author's aforesaid warranties and indemnities to any person, firm, or corporation at any time and Author shall be liable thereon as if originally made to such person, firm, or corporation.

BREACH OF WARRANTY

In the event of a breach of any of Author's warranties or any default by Author in the performance of his indemnities, Publisher may at its election and without prejudice to any other right or remedy against Author terminate this Agreement and in such event Author shall repay on demand to Publisher any advance against earnings or other sums paid to Author by Publisher.

From your publisher's point of view these are, perhaps, the most important clauses in the contract. When you sign the contract, you promise to indemnify the publisher and assume responsibility for the contents of your book. Authors have long felt that these clauses are unfair, that publishers should assume an equal responsibility. Many publishers are now offering free comprehensive liability insurance in the event suit is brought against them or the author and further, if the plaintiff is awarded damages for libel, slander, invasion of privacy, plagiarism, copyright infringement, or unfair competition.

There is usually an initial deductible provision in the insurance policy—this varies from publisher to publisher—but the author and the publisher will share any such costs up to approximately $25,000; beyond that figure, the insurance policy will cover further losses. The insurance coverage, however, does not relieve authors of responsibility, but it does protect them financially against unreasonable suits.

COPYRIGHT

(a) Publisher shall take out copyright in name of . . . and take all steps required to secure said copyright in the United States, and is authorized in its discretion to take out copyright in such other countries as may be covered by this Agreement. Author agrees to apply for the renewal of said copyrights on the expiration of the first term thereof, and authorizes Publisher to make such application in his name. Author further agrees to assign to Publisher, if this agreement has not terminated previously, the sole and exclusive right to print, publish, copy, and vend the work, and the other rights referred to herein, during the full term of said renewal and extensions thereof, on the same terms and conditions as for the original copyright term.

(b) Author hereby authorizes Publisher to make Author a co-plaintiff with Publisher in any litigation against a third party for infringement of the copyright on the work, but without cost to Author. Any recovery from such litigation shall be applied first to reimburse Publisher for its expenses in connection therewith, and the balance shall be divided equally between Author and Publisher.

(c) Author agrees that in the event the present copyright law of the United States of America or of any other country where the work is protected by copyright shall be amended or changed or a new copyright law is enacted so that the term of copyright is extended or the benefits thereunder enlarged, Publisher shall forthwith automatically become entitled to all of such enlarged benefits thereby conveyed for such extended term.

Although writers can copyright their own work directly with the Register of Copyrights at the Library of Congress, it is usual for the publisher to apply for copyright on behalf of an author. The copyright notice—Copyright © 198–, Author's Name—will appear in every copy of every edition of your book all over the world. Copyright is your protection against claims, misuse, plagiarism, infringement and unfair quotation without permission. Copyright of any title extends to 50 years after the death of an author, and, at that time, will fall into public domain.

REMAINDERS

If Publisher has a stock on hand which, in its judgment, could not be sold on usual terms in a reasonable time, it may sell such copies to any purchaser or purchasers, including Publisher's subsidiaries, at the best price it can secure. If such stock is sold at or below Publisher's cost, no royalty shall be paid to Author on such sales. If such copies are sold above Publisher's cost, the royalty paid to Author (in lieu of the royalty set forth in Paragraph 3 hereof) shall be ten per cent (10%) of the revenue obtained from such sales.

If your book is no longer selling enough copies to be profitable, the publisher has the right to sell off remaining copies in stock to an outside party who, in all likelihood, will turn around and sell them at considerable discount to bookstores who sell at a discount. If the publisher realizes a profit on the sale, the author is paid a reduced royalty of 10% of whatever amount the publisher receives. The author will also have the opportunity, before the remainder sale is made, to purchase directly from the publisher at cost as many copies as are available.

Most contracts do not limit the time when remaindering may take place but it is advisable, and often possible, to insert an addition to this clause which states: "No remaindering shall take place sooner than one year following first publication, and not unless sales in the preceding six (6) month period are less than 1,000 copies."

The publisher might not agree to a particular number of book sales—1,000 copies, or 2,500, or 1,500— but he will usually agree not to remainder your book within the first year after publication. The remainder clause is less important in paperback. Original paperbacks are not usually remaindered; if they don't sell, they are returned to the publisher and often pulped so that the paper can be used again.

COPIES OF SUB-AGREEMENTS
Publisher undertakes, upon request, to furnish to Author verified copies of any agreements which Publisher may make with any third party for the disposition of any rights in the work.

Not all contracts have this clause, but it is a reasonable request of your publisher. If it's not in your contract, ask to have it included. You will want to know what arrangements your publisher may make with a reprint publisher, a book club and for other subsidiary sales.

BANKRUPTCY
In case of bankruptcy, receivership, or assignment for benefit of creditors of Publisher, the right of publication shall revert to Author and thereupon this Agreement shall terminate but Author shall have the right to buy back any remaining copies or sheets at a fair market value, to be determined by agreement.

Publishers sometimes do go bankrupt, and if your contract does not contain this clause it can be added, usually without any problem, as a rider to the contract.

RIGHTS NOT SPECIFIED
All rights not herein specifically granted to Publisher are reserved by Author.

Many contracts don't have this "reservation of rights clause." You never know what's going to happen in the future and you can suggest to your publisher that it be included. This protects the author and guarantees that any profits realized from publication or use in any form, now known or unknown (cable TV, satellite transmission, etc.) will be shared with you.

OPTION
Author hereby agrees that Publisher shall have the first option to

publish Author's next full-length book, but in no case shall Publisher be required to exercise this option within three months following publication of the work which is the subject of this Agreement.

This is a straightforward option clause. The only change I would suggest for my authors is that they not have to wait *three months following publication* for the publisher to decide whether or not he is going to make an offer on the author's next work. The maximum I would accept is *three months following acceptance* of the current work. I would also suggest that the next work be considered on the basis of a proposal and possibly two chapters rather than a complete manuscript.

Many option clauses are much more detailed and complicated:

"The Author agrees to submit in writing the Author's Next Work (as defined below) for publication by the Publisher before soliciting offers from other Publishers. The Publisher shall be entitled to a period of thirty (30) days after receipt of the submission (which thirty (30)-day period shall not commence in any event before the end of ninety (90) days after publication of the Work by the Publisher) in which to notify the Author of whether it will exercise its option with respect to the Next Work. If within that time the Publisher shall notify the Author that it is exercising its option, the Author and the Publisher shall thereupon enter into negotiations towards an agreement concerning that Next Work. If the Publisher and the Author shall be unable within an additional sixty (60) days after the end of such thirty (30) days to arrive at a mutually satisfactory agreement, the Author shall be free to submit that Next Work elsewhere"—*and this is where it be-*

gins to get particularly onerous—"provided, however, that the Author shall not in any event enter into a contract for the publication of that Next Work with any other publisher upon the same terms or upon terms less favorable to the Author than those offered by the Publisher, or enter into a contract for publication of that Next Work on terms more favorable to the Author than those offered by the Publisher without first giving the Publisher a further option to enter into a contract as favorable to the Author as that offered by the other publisher, such further option shall be exercised by giving notice to the Author at any time within thirty (30) days of the Author giving written notice to the Publisher of the offer."

This is called a matching option, and it can tie an author up for quite a long time. Not only would I ask for consideration of the Next Work after *acceptance* of the first, rather than after *publication* and include language to the effect that the publisher would consider a proposal and two chapters, but I would also negotiate an even more vital concession: that the publisher eliminate the further option period. If an author receives an offer from another publisher on his next book, the publisher of the author's first book has an option to make a counter offer within a period of thirty days. The second publisher is not likely to wait for the first publisher to make up his mind; if the first publisher has not been able to agree upon terms with an author by this time, he's unlikely to do so later. In my view, this kind of option inhibits the author's ability to negotiate freely.

Although it is not always possible to get the "matching option" part of this clause removed entirely, it is sometimes possible to amend it so that the publisher must make a counter offer within two or three business days or offer an additional 10% above the offer of the second publisher.

When authors read a publisher's contract for the first time, they should keep in mind that some of the clauses are negotiable. Even if you are a first-time author, you do not have to accept everything as it is outlined by the publisher. You can ask questions and make some changes, and you should understand exactly what you're selling. If you don't understand some of the points in your contract, you should discuss them with your editor or agent. Don't be intimidated by it and don't sign it until you understand it completely and agree to it.

Publishers are not out to take advantage of authors; they are, however, protecting themselves. It's your responsibility to make sure that points that can protect you are included, or amended, in the contract. And it is your agent's job to see that you are protected and will be compensated for your work to the greatest possible extent.

XII

THE PUBLISHING PROCESS

SIGNING A NEW CONTRACT with a publisher is a time of enormous optimism and pleasure; the agony and disappointments of finding an agent or selling your manuscript are over, and it's time to celebrate. You will probably have revisions to make or rewriting on your manuscript, but you're not alone now—you have the support and interest of an editor to help you along.

At the same time you will begin to lose some control of your manuscript; your publisher has bought the right to print, market and publish it, and now other people begin to form opinions and make decisions about it. Publishers don't buy books with the idea that every one is going to be a runaway best seller. They buy books because they like the ideas or the stories; because they fit into the overall scope of their list; they know the audience for your book, and they anticipate making a profit. It may be a modest profit, but certainly one which will add to their overall financial benefit.

The author's first, and often only, contact with his publishing company will be the editor who works on

113

his or her manuscript. In most cases, the editor who buys your book is the editor you'll be working with as you complete or revise your manuscript. Sometimes a senior or acquiring editor will have bought your manuscript and another editor is actually assigned to work on it with you.

Your editor is your advocate within the company. When an editor receives your manuscript on submission, he reads and likes it, and then he has to sell it to his own company. Every editor has the power to reject a manuscript he or she doesn't like; very few have the power to buy manuscripts without the approval of an editorial board or editor-in-chief.

The decision-making editorial board is composed not only of the publisher and editor-in-chief but of the heads of marketing, advertising, sales, publicity and subsidiary rights, many of whom will not have read your manuscript or proposal but only *about* it. When an editor likes a manuscript and wants to buy it, he has to gather support from his colleagues, work out a profit and loss statement—how much the book will cost to produce, how many copies have to be sold to make a profit—write a proposal that includes a description of the book, the author's qualifications, the reasons for publishing this book, and an analysis of the potential market. Before an editor takes the step of making a proposal to the board he will have discussed your manuscript and his opinion of it at a weekly editorial meeting. This is a meeting of editors at which ideas and new manuscripts are discussed. By the time an editor's proposal reaches the editorial board, there will be a general awareness of the manuscript and its possibilities. An editor's proposal to buy—his report, the profit and loss statement, sometimes colleagues' supporting reports, all relevant information—is usually circulated to the editorial board the week before it will be discussed. Some boards make the decision on the proposal alone; sometimes the originating editor can also make a verbal presentation or sometimes his department head will.

Often a decision not to make an offer, which can happen even if an editor spent weeks putting his proposal together, has less to do with the manuscript than with the mood of the board that morning or the overall plans of the company, or their commitments for that season or month.

By the time an offer is made, your editor is not only pleased to be making it, but relieved that all the time and energy he has invested in your manuscript has produced a positive result. By now, your manuscript has also become your editor's, and his conviction and enthusiasm are going to help carry it through to successful publication.

Being an editor is not the leisurely profession it was when Maxwell Perkins worked with Thomas Wolfe. Editors work on several manuscripts at once; they're always getting ready for their next list, signing up books for the future, keeping on top of books about to be published, attending sales conferences, subsidiary rights and marketing meetings, reading new manuscripts and, in between all of these daily activities, editing.

Your manuscript might not need much discussion and editing, but even so you will want to feel that your editor is in tune with what you're doing, that he has ideas and insights that can make a difference to the work you produce. Your editor's job is not to rewrite your manuscript, or even to impose his point of view, but rather to help you see that within the scope of your work, its themes and ideas are clearly organized, that it works structurally, that it doesn't leave unanswered questions. A good editor is a good reader who can articulate what he or she likes or does not like about your work, what is effective and what isn't. If an editor can help you see your own work clearly and with a fresh eye, you will, if it's necessary, be open to rewriting, restructuring and rethinking your manuscript until it's the best that it can be.

As an author you should be open to your editor's suggestions and ideas. Editors and writers are not always entirely sure about what's right or wrong or what's most effective, but a good editor/writer relationship is one in which, through listening to each other, through a process of discussion, compromise and negotiation, they make the manuscript stronger and better than it was before.

The focus of your relationship with your editor is your manuscript. It can be very intense and exciting when you're working together either through correspondence or personally, but when it's finally as good as it can be and it goes into production, you may feel a bit let down. There's nothing for you to do but wait (and publication itself is probably eight or nine months away), your editor is not quite so available, you don't get reports as often. The first weeks of being in production are slow for an author, and it seems as if nothing is happening, but in fact your editor is now dealing with all the other departments that will be involved in the production and publication of your book—art, design, subsidiary rights, publicity, marketing all begin to form their plans.

Several things begin to happen when your manuscript is completed. A copy goes into the production department, where the process of translating your manuscript into a book begins. A word count is done, which translates into the number of pages. A designer begins to work on the kind of type that will be used, the size of type, what kind of headings will be used, the quality and weight of paper, and the binding. Your editor probably knows before he sends your manuscript into production how he wants your book to look; he will discuss all the elements and possibilities with production and they will make it work. Your editor will have a meeting with the art director, and they'll discuss both the feeling that they want and how that might be made to work on the jacket. The art director will hire a free-lance graphic designer to create the cover. Your editor is intimately involved with the physical appearance of your book, and although you won't have final approval (this is ultimately a marketing decision), you will have discussed your ideas with your editor.

Soon after your manuscript is in production your editor will receive a schedule which will tell her when the copy-edited manuscript is due, when galleys will be ready, what the book date is and what official publication date will be. While the designer is working on the inside appearance, the art director with the jacket, a copy editor will be going through your manuscript for consistency of style, facts, grammar and repetitions. When your manuscript has been copy edited, it will be returned to you for a final check. At this point you can agree or disagree with any copy editing changes. It is also the last chance you will have to make any additions or deletions that are more than minor; it's your last chance to make real changes in the text of your work.

The next time you see it, it won't be in manuscript form but set in type on long "galleys." At this point any major changes become expensive—you'll see a clause in your contract that states that changes amounting to more than 10% of the text have to be paid for by you. At the galley stage you will be checking that the printer hasn't made errors and that the text is accurate.

On the schedule your editor receives from the production department is something called "book date." This is the day your book comes off the presses. Your editor will probably receive a couple of early copies, one of which will be sent to you. The finished copies of the book will now be shipped from the printer to the publisher's warehouse, and from there to bookstores and jobbers all over the country.

It used to be that books couldn't be sold or reviewed before the publisher's publication date, but now books are sold and reviewed as soon as they're available. Publication date now means that your book is available in every area of the country and that initial orders have been filled.

As soon as your manuscript is in production, your editor will send a copy to his subsidiary rights department. Even if you have an agent handling first serial, foreign and film rights, your publisher will be selling book club and reprint rights. Book clubs will be the first priority. Is it for the Literary Guild or Book-of-the-Month Club? Is it for a more specialized club?

If your book is hardcover, the decision about reprint has to be made. Should it be sold before or after publication? If there's a book club sale, if the agent's sold first serial rights to a major magazine, if there are foreign sales, perhaps there's enough energy generated by the book to interest reprinters before publication. If these things aren't happening or if the publisher is expecting good review attention when the book is published, the decision might be made to wait until after publication to offer reprint rights.

Everything that happens to your book happens through your editor. He doesn't make all the decisions but he is part of the decision-making process with all the people and departments involved in producing and publishing your book.

If you have an agent you'll probably find yourself talking to him more often than you will your editor. Your agent will be supportive and, if you don't hear from your editor as frequently as you'd like, your agent will call to find out what's happening to your manuscript. Your agent's role does not end with the signing of the contract. Agents have continuing and good relationships with editors, and it is their responsibility to keep on top of things. A good agent is a partner with the editor and writer in the process of publication.

XIII

MARKETING YOUR BOOK

BOOKS ARE published in seasons. While many publishers have two selling seasons, some break their year into three sections. Basically, however, spring and summer books are sold in the winter, and fall and winter books in the summer.

Whether a publishing house has its own salaried sales people, commissioned representatives, or a combination of both, every publisher holds sales conferences at which the editorial department presents its books to the sales department.

If your book is being published in March, it will be presented at the sales meeting held the previous December, which covers the March through August list. Either your editor or his editorial director will make a verbal presentation to the sales people. The presentation is also written up and included in a sales kit, which also includes jackets and other information that can help the sales person sell your book to the bookstore buyers. Your editor will have two or three minutes to describe your book, talk about you, give the book a "sales handle"—that is, one line that conveys the sense and scope of your book—possible sales angles and markets, and any early reactions, such as a book club sale or early endorsements from other writers. Your editor may be presenting as many as nine or ten books, and there will be other editors presenting their books. When the formal presentations are ended, the editors and sales people have a chance to relax and discuss their lists more informally. However, it's a high-pressure situation; your editor has to make your book stand out so the people who will be selling to the stores will take note of it.

The sales department weighs the information they've heard about the books coming up on the next list, and each sales person offers his or her own opinion about potential sales and determines how many copies of each title they think they can place with the stores and chains in their territory. In this way, an "advance" sale is established. If it's a first novel, sales people will be cautious; they might expect to place only one or two copies in some of their stores, perhaps a few hundred with B. Dalton and Waldenbooks (these are bookstore chains with outlets all over the country), and the final tally might produce a projected advance of 6,000 copies. If the new book is by a well-known author with a strong sales record for his or her previous books, the advance sales projection can be based on those figures. At this point, the sales department is really establishing its own quota. Their job, once the sales conference is over, is to return to the territories they cover, visit the buyers and sell the list to meet the sales quotas they've established. Years of experience go into thinking and knowing which store will take how many copies of any given title. The publisher's sales force knows the buyers, their interests, their clientele, what sells well in certain areas, what won't. A good sales person will not force a store to take more copies of any title than the buyer thinks will sell. Overselling (and buying) only invites returns, which are not profitable for anyone—author, store, or publisher.

Books are sold by publishers to bookstores at discounts which vary, depending upon whether the store chooses a full refund policy or not—that is, the publisher buys back books already shipped and paid for if the store doesn't sell them. Stores can get bigger discounts from publishers if they agree to a partial or non-refundable policy.

Deciding how many copies of a title are to be printed is tricky and important. A publisher does not want to overprint and have copies returned or held in stock; it's too expensive. And he doesn't want to print too few copies in case there's a demand for the book which he can't fill fast enough. It can take from three weeks to three months to print a new edition of a book. The number of copies of your book printed is a minimum expectation. As the sales people go out to sell, they gauge the reaction of the buyers, and sometimes advance sales come in higher or lower than anticipated. As advance orders flow into the publisher, the first print run is established. If an advance has been set at 7,500 copies and the orders are coming in at that level, the first printing might be put at 10,000 copies. If the advance orders are not as strong as expected, the first printing may be reduced to 6,000 copies.

Editors are sometimes cautious about giving authors

information about advance sales, but about six or eight weeks before your book date, the information should start coming in. This is where reality begins to set in. Until now you and your editor, and agent if you have one, have been concentrating on the manuscript and less on the marketplace and what is going to happen when your book is published. As you approach publication you will be more interested in the number of copies to be printed, what kind of advertising your book will receive and how the publisher plans to promote you and your book.

There's a continual discussion within publishing about advertising. Authors say, "If you don't advertise my book how will anyone know it exists?" Publishers say, "Advertising doesn't help unless there are good reviews, subsidiary sales and a strong indication that the book is selling."

The publisher's opinion usually prevails. Most books published are not, in fact, advertised in the general press. Your book may receive an announcement ad in *Publishers Weekly,* sometimes as part of a complete list, or perhaps half or a third of a page. Your book might appeal to a special market—finance or gardening, perhaps—and the publishers may place an ad in a magazine catering to audiences interested in those subjects. It's not that publishers don't want to sell your book; but sometimes a book isn't generating enough cash, and the fact is that they really do believe that advertising doesn't help sell a book unless it's already selling.

Then, of course, there is publicity. This involves not only having an author appear on talk shows (The Today Show, Phil Donahue, etc.). It includes getting galleys or bound books to reviewers, thinking of and placing possible feature articles and stories about the author in particular newspapers or magazines; sometimes writing those features and sending them to columnists, journalists, and local publications with which the author or the subject has some connection. Seeing the angle that might work on local television, trying to put a group of writers with similar concerns together as a "package" for presentation to discussion programs—all of this and lots more goes into "publicity." And if the author is well known, and has a pleasing personality, and for whose book the publisher has high hopes, he or she may be sent on a promotion tour to a number of cities—at the publisher's expense, sometimes with an "advance publicity person" to see that the schedules work out.

If publicity works, if items are picked up by papers and magazines, if people begin to talk about a book, sales will increase and advertising will follow.

Long before your book is published, you will receive a publicity questionnaire from the publicity department of your publisher. You will be asked for basic information such as your name and address and where you went to school, are you married, do you have children. You will also be asked to give:

A brief summary of principal occupations
Other fields of interest or study
A list of places you've lived for any length of time
Other locations that may have a special interest in you
Countries in which you've traveled or lived

Organizations and societies to which you belong
Other publications—books or articles
A description of your book in 200 words
Information about your writing habits
Other writing plans
Points you feel should be stressed in selling your book
Other books that compare or compete with yours
A list of people or publications who you know might help
    in selling your book through reviews or articles
A brief biographical resume including anecdotes

Every book has a publicity release written for it. This, together with a copy of the galleys (for major review media only) or an early copy of the book and perhaps an author photo, is sent to book reviewers all over the country. The first review copies are sent by the publishers to *Publishers Weekly,* where a relatively small number of selected titles are reviewed in the Forecast section—very influential with bookstores and libraries; to *The Kirkus Reviews,* a trade reviewing service to which libraries, publishers, and bookstores subscribe and which gives acerbic, opinionated but often insightful appraisals of books; and *The Library Journal,* which publishes thoughtful reviews and is primarily a buying guide for librarians (and an important source of sales). The ALA *Booklist,* a very influential journal for librarians, also publishes reviews in their "Upfront" section. These four journals all give reviews well in advance of dates of publication.

Publicity departments of publishing houses also want to know about any possible regional interest in your book, either because of its content or you. Very often interest built regionally can be catapulted into national attention.

Not every book lends itself to every kind of publicity. Some books will receive review attention, others won't get reviewed but will receive off-the-book-page interviews with the author, or perhaps on local television and radio. Novelists have a harder time on the air than do authors of nonfiction. It's hard for an interviewer to carry on an interesting conversation with a novelist, but a nonfiction book on practically any topic provides an excellent basis for discussion and information.

As an author with a new book, you will find there's a limit to what your publisher's publicity department can, or will, do for your book. National publicity tours are given to the big books and big names because that's what the national shows want. You will probably have several good ideas about publicizing your book. If your publisher doesn't pick up on those ideas, do it yourself—call newspapers, write to reviewers, check your local television and radio stations, visit local bookstores. It is possible to do some of your own publicity and it can help.

Publicity about a book usually appears within the first three months of publication, and by then you will have a clear idea of how your book is doing—whether it's still in the stores, whether it is selling in the bookstores, whether you're getting good review coverage—but the first hard information you are likely to receive will be in your first royalty statement. It may very well arrive without a royalty check. First of all, sales from your book have to recoup its advance. This might have been helped along by subsidiary sales, but because it is early in your book's life, your publisher will be holding a reserve against returns. Also, the statement covers the six-month period which ended three months earlier and new sales aren't accounted for in this statement. Your second royalty statement will be more informative about your book's status, and may even include a check.

Royalty statements are often confusing. All of them tell you the number of copies sold within the given period, whether they are paying the full royalty, whether it's a discount royalty from special sales, whether any subsidiary monies have been paid. But every publisher has a different format and the information itself is skimpy. If you don't understand your royalty statement, ask your agent or editor to explain it to you. Often you will find that they don't know the answers either, and they will have to consult the royalty department. Checking royalty statements annoys everyone because it's time-consuming, tedious, and never seems to make real sense, but don't give up. Publishers do sometimes make mistakes.

The best thing about publishing is that every book is a different experience for the editor and for everyone else who works on each title. People work for publishing companies, or as agents, because they like books and authors, because books are special to them, because books make a difference to the quality of their lives. While publishers must be responsive to the marketplace, the decision to publish a book or not is, first of all, a subjective decision. Once an agent, editor, and publisher decide that they like a manuscript, want to work with the author and publish the book, they have to find ways to sell it. Not every book is a great book or will become a classic, but the publication of every book does take commitment and enthusiasm and sometimes even passion. Being an author is often frustrating, but it's worth knowing when you sit down to write every day that there are thousands of people in publishing who think that books are special, who are looking for writers with fresh ideas and great imaginations.

INDEX

129